Wrote a book? et Published" gives ...at happen — from co... it. This book is a practical guide to becoming a published author from an insider who understands how the business works.

Joan Livingston, best-selling author of the Isabel Long Mystery Series and Editor-in-Chief at Greenfield Recorder, Massachusetts, USA

"Let's Get Published! It does what it says on the cover-page. No frills, no nonsense, just the very latest advice from an author who is currently in the thick of it. I have around a dozen books in publication. The advice I had when I began is already out of date. Val Penny tells how it's done NOW! There are eight books on getting published on my bookshelves. I am about to replace them all with this one! I write professionally and tutor three writing groups. I will be recommending *Let's Get Published* to all my students. Easy to follow, interesting and - most importantly in this rapidly changing industry - *current* advice on getting published. Val Penny hasn't just been there, she is still out there at the creative cutting edge."

David McLaughlan - top selling author and 'Francis Gay' of The Sunday Post, Scotland

"If you're interested in writing a book, and getting published, this guide is indispensable. It takes you through everything you need to know to write a successful novel and experience the joy of seeing it on the shelves. It's thorough, comprehensive, but also accessible and realistic. It doesn't gloss over the fact that writing is very hard work sometimes, but it also balances that viewpoint with an important truth: That it's incredibly rewarding. Val is a writer I know well, who has worked hard to become a success, and is now making another excellent contribution to the publishing and writing world by helping others follow in her footsteps."

Simon Hall – best selling author of the TV Detective Novels and Lecturer at Cambridge University, England

"Let's Get Published is an essential read for any writers wishing to 'get published'. As Val Penny notes 'becoming a successful author is not easy' but armed with this inspirational guide, any writer will have a formidable ally with them on their writing journey."

Fiona Samuel, teacher, editor and author, England

'An insightful read, full of interesting content and helpful advice. A great starting point for anyone looking to publish their first book.'

Lizzie Chantree, best selling author of 'If You Love Me, I'm Yours', England

Let's Get Published

Bestselling Author of The Edinburgh Crime Mysteries

Val Penny

Books by Val Penny

Fiction
The Edinburgh Crime Mysteries
Hunter's Chase
Hunter's Revenge
Hunter's Force
Hunter's Blood
and coming soon
Hunter's Secret

Non-Fiction
Let's Get Published

To Dave, thank you

Acknowledgements

I am very grateful to Laurence Paterson of for his assistance and guidance in putting this book together, my friends Avril Rennie, Allison Symes and David MacLauchlan. For their unswerving encouragement.   And I am also, as always, indebted to my beloved husband. His patience, support and silence have been most helpful in putting this work together.

Most of all, I am grateful to my each one of my readers. I hope this book will be useful to those of you looking towards a career as an author.

About the Author

Val Penny is an American author living in SW Scotland. She has two adult daughters of whom she is justly proud and lives with her husband and two cats. She has a Law degree from Edinburgh University and her MSc from Napier University. She has had many jobs including hairdresser, waitress, lawyer, banker, azalea farmer and lecturer. However, she has not yet achieved either of her childhood dreams of being a ballerina or owning a candy store. Until those dreams come true, she has turned her hand to writing poetry, short stories and novels.

Her crime novels, 'Hunter's Chase' Hunter's Revenge, Hunter's Force and Hunter's Blood form the bestselling series The Edinburgh Crime Mysteries. They are set in Edinburgh, Scotland, published by Crooked Cat Books. The fifth novel in the series, Hunter's Secret, is published by darkstroke and available to pre-order now. This book is her first non-fiction book.

Let's Get Published

Contents

Chapter One

Introduction

Many people say *anybody can write a book.* Most of these individuals have never tried to write one. Alternatively, it is often said that *everybody has a book inside of them.* That is simply not true. This is repeated and belittles the achievements of authors.

In truth, it is a very hard thing to write a book. Most people never attempt it, fewer still succeed in getting published. But if you have written a novel, or novella, or perhaps compiled a collection of short stories, poems or flash fiction, this book may help you with the next step. It is primarily intended for authors of fiction who have completed a draft of their novel and who are now looking to prepare it for submission to agents or publishers.

Of course, it may also aid poets, short story writers and authors of non-fiction. It is designed to facilitate authors maximise their success when submitting work to agents or publishers. It is to help authors consider their priorities and preferences for getting work into print and identify the agents and/or publishers they want to approach. It should also assist with editing their manuscript fully prior to submission and preparing their submission package to give them the best chance of success.

Writing a novel is hard work.

Completing even the first rough draft of a novel can take months or even years, particularly if you're trying to fit your writing in amongst work or other commitments. It is definitely a marathon, not a sprint and requires dedication and persistence. The American writer Richard Bach who is widely known as the author of some of the 1970s' biggest sellers, including Jonathan Livingston Seagull once said,

'A professional writer is an amateur who didn't quit'.

If you have finished the first draft of your novel and, like all writers, you now want it to reach the widest possible readership. It has to be published so that other people can read your book and enjoy the fruits of your labour.

Getting your book published is likely to be even harder work than writing it. We have all heard the stories of the multiple rejections received by now best-selling authors including Kathryn Stockett who wrote *The Help*, also Stephen King's bestselling novel, *Carrie*, was rejected over thirty times and even J.K. Rowling's *Harry Potter* novels were rejected on numerous occasions before Bloomsbury took a chance on *Harry Potter and the Philosopher's Stone*. No matter how good your book might be, to get it published you will need the same level of determination, resilience, hard work and careful planning that you harnessed to write it.

Nevertheless, there is good news. There are now more routes to publication than ever before. Even just a few years ago, the market was dominated by a small number of publishing houses, most of which refused to consider any submission that was not made by a literary agent. Then, most literary agents either had full client lists and, if they did not, they were loath to take on new or unknown authors.

This situation has changed dramatically. Of course, the major publishing houses still exist, but even their attitude to agents and new authors has mellowed. Many of them now have imprints that accept submissions direct from the author. In addition to this there is a growing number of independent publishers. Most of these accept either agented or unagented submissions. They take advantage of the comparatively low costs available when publishing and distributing e-books, in preference to or as well as often offering paperbacks, on a print on demand basis. This model allows the independent publishers to provide a more responsive and faster service both to their authors and readers.

There are even publishers offering more innovative ways of supporting publication. These methods include crowdfunding. This can be particularly useful for books that are quite specialist or have niche appeal.

If all that were not enough, there is also the option of self-publishing. Years ago, this was the Cinderella method of publishing. It was considered the last resort for those authors unable to obtain a conventional publishing deal. In recent years this has changed dramatically. There have been increasing instances of high-quality authors opting to self-publish, many do so most successfully. A number of these writers are new authors who have opted for this route. Some of the others are authors who have previously been conventionally published but have written a different genre of book or are just seeking a more flexible approach. A growing number of hybrid authors combine conventional publication and self-publishing to best develop their writing careers.

Chapter Two

Your Book

Every author must know what kind of book they have written and who their intended audience is. So now, identify the genre of the book you have written and consider where it will fit into the market.

If your novel is commercial fiction think about whether it fits into an established genre. There are many sub-genres and crossover genre but consider the main genre that encompasses your work.

Here are some of the most common examples of genres fiction:

* Children's fiction
* Comedy
* Crime
* Fantasy
* Historical
* Horror
* Romance
* Romantic comedy
* Sagas
* Thriller
* Women's fiction
* Young Adult

Most of these genres can be broken down into sub-genres. For example, within crime fiction, the sub genres include cosy crime, hard-boiled crime, psychological thrillers, police procedurals, and tartan noir. Literary fiction has not been included as a genre because, strictly speaking, it can encompass a wide range of subjects. The basic distinction between literary and commercial fiction is widely considered and primarily reflects a difference in market and readership. When you are considering agents or publishers, bear in mind that they tend to specialise in either commercial or in literary fiction and are unlikely to be interested in both.

If you can honestly say that your novel falls squarely into one specific genre, it will be easier to identify agents and publishers who are most likely to be interested in it. Many publishers specialise only in a particular genre. Also, larger publishers often have imprints for specific genres. Others are open to a broader range of commercial genre fiction. Likewise, when you are seeking an agent, do check that the agent of your choice specifies an interest in your genre.

However, it may be that your novel does not fit neatly into a single genre. This is not really a problem. There are many successful novels that cross genres. Indeed, those such as fantasy crime, paranormal crime, historical crime and historical romance are now well established.

You do need to be aware that the harder it is to categorise your book, the more difficulty you may have in persuading an agent to represent you or a publisher to accept it. Agents and publishers try to be open-minded about genre, particularly if they are enthusiastic about a book, but they will undoubtedly consider the difficulty of persuading readers to try something unfamiliar. Therefore, if your book does not fall neatly into a category, as an author, you may find it harder to offer a clear and concise way of explaining your work to potential agents, publishers and even readers.

Sometimes, if you find it difficult to categorise your book, it may be helpful to identify its similarities to books by authors who are already published or even individual books. You can tell agents or publishers which works yours most resembles. It

9

can be easiest to use the formula employed by publishers to market books.

'If you enjoyed that book - then this new book is for you.'

Give some thought as to the readers your book is aimed at and will appeal to most readily. Think about what else they are likely to be reading and bring to mind other authors they will be likely to enjoy. This is not to suggest that your novel is derivative or that it is not original, but to make you think about the readership that will be likely to appreciate your book.

So, consider similarities in terms of subject-matter, style, characters or even setting. This way you will identify several comparable authors. After this you can research who represents or publishes them and check what other books are on that agent or publisher's list. Picture whether your novel would sit comfortably there.

Beta readers are another great source of assistance at this stage. When you give your completed draft to those whom you trust to give full and honest feed-back, you should seek their views as to the other books or authors that it reminds them of. Ask them which readers it is most likely to appeal to. You can also ask them, if they enjoyed your book, what other authors or novels they read. This is valuable research in a safe environment which will stand you in good stead when you dive into the wild world of publishing.

Chapter Three

Your Ambitions and Aspirations

As an author, you need to think about why you want to be published. You must think about your aspirations and why you want your book to be in print. What realistic outcomes do you want from the publication of your work.

At the point when your book is complete, it is easy to think of its publication as an aim in its own right. After all, you have put in all that hard work, so, clearly, the novel should be published. However, in practice, writers often have a variety of reasons for wanting to see their book printed.

* Become famous
* Be widely read
* Build a career as an author
* Make money

Realistically, most authors include a combination of some or all of these aims. Nevertheless, it is always worth considering your priorities.

If you want to write a bestselling novel, then you must ensure that your book appeals to one of the large publishers. If you are happy to have your work read and appreciated on a more modest scale, you might submit to a smaller or more specialist publisher. This will really depend in part on the book you have written. If you have written a tense, historical romance, you may hope to have a best seller on your hands. But if your book is about the development of the lightbulb, your work will doubtless be better suited to a niche publisher.

11

So, consider the publication route you would prefer. To do this accurately, list your motivations and then try to put them in priority order, with 1 being the highest priority and 5 being the lowest.

Nobody should become an author with the aim of getting rich. The writers who make a lot of money form only a fraction of authors who are published. They are not only very talented but have experienced an unusual amount of luck. Most authors earn less than the average wage from their writing. Even some well-known writers earn too little to live on and must supplement their income with other work. This is sometimes writing related, sometimes not. For example, David McLaughlan (Francis Gay of the Sunday Post), supplements his income by tutoring creative writing while crime writer Amit Dhand works full time as a pharmacist.

Any options you have for publishing your novel will most likely depend on your aspirations for wanting to write. If you want to build a career as an author, you must be thoroughly committed to that end. You will require the time, determination and ability to write several books. You should aim to publish at least one book a year. You must build yourself and your novels into a *brand*. This must be recognisable to the public. To this end, you must write novels that are broadly similar in style and content. Typically, that means your novels will sit within the same genre. You want to write books that attract readers to choose your novels because your name is on the cover and they trust you to produce the type of story that they will enjoy. This is hard work. It requires you to have commitment to your craft, treat your writing as a business and a long-term perspective to build your *brand*.

If you want to produce bestsellers, you will have to be prepared to do what is required to promote yourself and your books. It is increasingly difficult for writers to remain writing in an attic or tapping on their keyboard. Even the largest publishers with the biggest budgets expect their authors actively to promote their books at book festivals, on social media and at promotional events.

To be successful, you will want to build a presence on social media, attend promotional events, and give interviews to the media. Your publisher may also want you to write articles or short stories and deliver talks or participate in discussions at book fairs, on radio, television or on podcasts. Many writers find this difficult. They are more comfortable being behind the scenes rather than being in front of an audience.

Conducting a book signing or speaking at your local library to the book group may be a gentle way to ease yourself into public speaking. These are much more enjoyable if you have a queue waiting or an audience than if you are sitting behind a desk firmly ignored by those going about their business. But often writers overcome their discomfort with public speaking and some even enjoy it enormously.

If you feel unable to publicise your novel or believe you will only want to write and publish one book that is fine. But it will influence your approach to publication. Some authors write books sporadically, think of Harper Lee who wrote the literary best seller, *To Kill a Mockingbird* in 1960 and did not publish the sequel, *To Set a Watchman* until 2015. So, should you consider yourself to be a writer who will only complete a book every ten years or more, like Donna Tartt, or perhaps you are a writer who simply wants to follow your own imagination without consideration of the market, then, again, think about this as you approach publishing your book. Perhaps you should consider a niche publisher, or even self-publishing your work. Be aware, though, that to be a successful self-published author you will require to undertake even more marketing and promotions.

Whatever the course you choose to pursue, it must be suitable for you. Each of the choices outlined reflects a legitimate preference and offers a route to aspirational success for an author. However, to achieve aspirational success you must be honest with yourself and have a clear understanding of your own motivations and objectives. This will help you target submissions to agents and publishers appropriately and increase your chances of achieving success.

Chapter Four

Routes to Publication

Consider now the advantages and disadvantages of some main routes to publication. These are the traditional large publisher, independent publisher, and self-publishing.

Traditional Large Publisher

<u>Advantages</u>

* Good distribution networks, which can get your book onto the shelves of bookshops
* Professional editing, production and cover design
* Professional marketing
* Can get your book reviewed in the media
* Can build a larger profile for the successful authors on their books than other forms of publishing
* Their higher profile is more likely to result in sale of overseas, audio and film/TV rights
* They still usually pay an *advance* to authors. This is an upfront payment which is then offset against future royalties.

<u>Disadvantages</u>
* Even with the biggest publishers, marketing spend on debut authors is small and you will require to make a considerable effort yourself to promote your book
* It is still difficult for debut authors to obtain bookshop space or reviews
* Traditional royalty payments for physical books are low, and traditional publishers have been slower to exploit the e-book market

* Most traditional publishers will not consider direct submissions, so you are unlikely to be accepted for publication by them without an agent

Independent Publisher

<u>Advantages</u>

* Move faster and are more responsive than traditional publishers. This means that the time from acceptance of your manuscript to publication of your book is shorter than with traditional publishers
* They are more flexible in accommodating highly productive authors who write more than one book a year.
* Effective at harnessing the benefits of social media. This includes Facebook groups, bloggers, Twitter, Instagram, podcasts and YouTube
* Build loyalty among readers to the publisher as well as individual authors
* Most focus primarily on the e-book market, paying high royalties to authors.
* Devote equivalent time and resources to all books they publish

<u>Disadvantages</u>

* Not having large resources nor as good media contacts as traditional publishers
* Do not focus on getting books into traditional bookshops
* Quality of editing, production and cover design may be lower
* Independent publishers do not offer an advance against royalties

Self Publishing

<u>Advantages</u>
* No entry barriers

* Costs are low and free support is available from distributors including Amazon
* You have full control over each process this includes cover design, marketing and pricing
* You receive all the royalties other than the production and distribution costs paid to the distributor
* It is easy to track your sales and income

Disadvantages

* You incur all editing, production and design costs. These are under your control and can be kept quite low, but they are payable up front
* Your novel will be one of many thousands published and so it is your responsibility to promote it
* Successful self-publishing requires your writing to be approached like a business and you will spend as much time marketing and promoting your book as writing the next one.

These comments are generalisations and the picture is constantly evolving. You, as an author, need to be aware of the commitment that will be required of you through the different methods of publication. Fellow author, Allison Symes once said:

'*You better like your first novel, because you'll be promoting it for the rest of your life!*'

The distinction between *traditional* and *independent* publishers is, however, becoming increasingly artificial. Many of the large publishers now have e-book or specific genre imprints which operate far more like independent publishers than its traditional parent. Equally, some independent publishers are now developing expertise to match those of their large, traditional cousins.

In order to decide where would be the best place to submit your novel, you need to consider the outcomes you want from

17

publication. If you put the following in order your priorities should help you decide whether you should target a traditional publisher, which means you require to find an agent first, an independent publisher, or whether you want to self-publish your work.

	Priority
Your book into book shops	
Your book reviewed in the media	
Selling printed books	
A large readership	
Maximise your income from your book	
An advance payment	
Control over publication	
Minimise the investment of your money in publication	
Minimise your time in marketing the book	

Chapter Five

What Everybody Wants

By now you should have clarified your objectives and priorities in your own mind. You know what you want so you must begin to research the market. A key question at this stage will be whether to approach literary agents or to focus only on publishers who will accept direct submissions. A few years ago, there would have been little choice. Most reputable publishers would not consider submissions except through agents, and it was virtually the only route to publication.

That has changed and continues to change. Many smaller publishers are keen to encourage direct submissions from authors, and some even prefer not to deal with agents. Many publishers now see this as a means of accessing a pool of writing talent which previously was excluded from the market. This picture will continue to change. Indeed, some have queried whether literary agents will continue to have a role in a more digital future. Of course, it may be that, if smaller publishers find themselves inundated with direct submissions, they will reintroduce some of the barriers used by the bigger firms.

This is not necessarily an either/or choice. There is nothing to stop you submitting your work to both agents and publishers. But, if you decide your priorities in advance, you are more likely to focus your efforts. The benefits and disadvantages of being represented by an agent are indicated here.

Benefits	Disadvantages
* Able to submit your work to larger, more traditional publishers who do not consider unagented submissions	* Will take a commission on your book earnings for their services
* Can provide up to date advice on the state of the market, e.g. what individual publishers are seeking, who is most likely to be interested in your work, and can target their submissions accordingly	* Cannot guarantee to sell your work (although being represented by an agent will significantly increase your chances of publication, agents do not always succeed)
* Can provide feedback on how to improve or change your work to make it most attractive to potential publishers	* The agent may become an additional *gatekeeper.* The agent will typically have signed you on the strength of one book, if they do not like your later manuscripts, they may become more of a barrier than a support
* Can negotiate deals on your behalf based on knowledge of the market	* Much will depend on your personal rapport with the agent. You need to be confident you can trust their judgment and that they act in your best interests.
* Can usually facilitate (either directly or through associates) foreign language and adaptation deals	

Even today, the best source of correct, up to date information about agents publishers and most other matters in the publishing world is still the *Writers' and Artists' Yearbook.* It is, as the title suggests, published every year and is an essential purchase for anyone intending to have their work published. It will help you to identify the publishers and agents who are most likely to be interested in your book. They indicate the genres and types of writing they are interested in and include examples of writers currently on their lists. Also, many explicitly state the genres or types of writing that they do *not* publish or represent, and this can also be useful. If you do not fit their criteria, there is no point in wasting your time and theirs.

Additionally, there are on-line tools available to help you search for agents and publishers. Many of these are free, others do require you to make a payment. These vary in their quality and usefulness. You may also get help and advice from writers' forums. These often document aspiring writers' experiences of approaching individual publishers or agents.

There are two particularly useful magazines in the United Kingdom: *Writers' Forum* and *Writing Magazine.* Also, in the United States of America, *The Writer* and *Writer's Digest*, are invaluable sources of information.

Take time at this point to research a list of agents and/or publishers that you believe might be useful to you going forward to get your book to the marketplace. Look carefully at the websites of the publishers and agents you have identified. This gives you full information about what they are looking for from you and what they offer to do. Of necessity, the information in the *Writers' and Artists' Yearbook*, is limited. Also, entries are submitted several months in advance, so checking the relevant websites helps to ensure you have the most contemporary information. It is always possible that circumstances and requirements for the agents or publishers you are researching may have changed. It is also worth looking at the agent's or publisher's social media profile, many are active on social media and you will get an up-to-date view of their interests and preferences. Think about the authors and books that are represented by the agents and publishers that you are researching and how your work would sit with them. Remember, the *fit* may be broader than a matter of genre. If your novel tells a *cosy crime* story, although it falls within the crime genre, it will not sit well in a list of *noir* crime fiction.

Agents and publishers provide their submission guidelines on their websites. It is your responsibility to read and follow these carefully. The first and most important question is whether they are currently accepting submissions. When an agent states that their list is currently closed or a publisher states that it does not accept open submissions, there is absolutely no point in submitting to them. Do not suppose that they will be so entranced by the individuality of your work that they will change their rules for you. It is not going to happen. The submission will, at best, be returned unread or, more likely, simply ignored.

Bear in mind that most traditional publishers do not accept unagented submissions. Therefore, if the publisher states in their submission guidelines that only submissions by agents will be accepted, they will not make an exception for your novel. However, some publishers do accept direct submissions. These are mostly the smaller, independent publishers. Many of them are actively seeking new authors to work with. Also, many traditional publishers are also looking to expand into the e-books market. For this, they often willing to accept unagented submissions, but this will usually be to their more newly established imprints.

It is also common for some agents and publishers only to open up submissions on a periodic basis. This enables them to cope with the expected volume of manuscripts submitted to them. Should the website state that they are closed to submissions but will re-open at a specified time it is important to make a note of the date as the windows are often quite short. Make sure your novel is completed to meet the timeframe window.

Chapter Six

Complete Your Manuscript

You have finished the first draft of your novel. This may seem like a basic issue but many authors looking to get their book published appear to believe that they will secure the representation of an agent, or get a publishing deal, even if they have only completed some of the chapters and the synopsis. While that might be possible, it is unusual. Any agent or publisher, even if they love your idea and your sample chapters, will require to see the whole manuscript.

The reasons for this are simple. They want evidence that your quality of writing is sustained throughout the novel. It is also important that they see you can properly plot and pace your book. You also need to prove to them that the character development and other aspects of writing a long piece of prose are within your capabilities. The agents and publishers must also know that you have the energy, commitment and resilience to finish a novel. Indeed, this last point may be the most crucial. There are few writers who have not written at least some chapters of a novel they have never finished.

To write a novel is an enormous commitment. This is especially true if, additionally, you have a full-time job or family commitments. No agent or publisher wants to make an offer unless they have evidence that you will complete the writing required of you within the time limits available.
When you think about how long your manuscript needs to be, there are many points to take into consideration and there is no one right answer to this question. It depends not only on the genre of the novel you are writing but also on your target audience.

For commercial adult fiction, such as crime or romance novels, most publishers will typically be looking for something in the order of 70,000-100,000 words. This allows the story to be properly told without it losing pace. Other genres, including science fiction or fantasy, which may require world building in addition to the tale being told, will probably be longer. For fiction aimed at younger readers, publishers will typically be looking for shorter manuscripts and the precise expectation of length will depend on the anticipated age range. If you are submitting a work of literary fiction, agents and publishers tend to accept a wide range of lengths. These vary from books little longer than novellas at 50,000 words to extremely long works of 200,000 words or sometimes even more.

In truth, a debut author will struggle to persuade any agent or publisher to accept a novel much more than 100,000 words long, unless the work is something exceptional. Check the submission guidelines as these may specify the minimum and maximum word count that agents or, even more particularly, publishers are willing to consider.

Of course, these traditional expectations of book length have been influenced by physical books. Purchasers browsing the shelves of a bookshop are more likely to be attracted to your book which, simply in terms of physical appearance, seems to offer good value for money without being unduly intimidating in length. One major commercial publisher considers the ideal length of book to be 95,000 words for this reason.

Because of this, several publishers, especially those who focus on e-books, are prepared to consider a flexible approach to the length of your novel. Naturally, customers who read e-books are much less focussed on the physical size of a book. Their reading progress is measured in percentage terms rather than page numbers. In any event, quality is always more important than quantity. But realistically, if you want to secure agent representation or a publishing deal, your first step must be to complete your book.

The first draft does not have to be perfect because any agent or publisher will have ideas as to how your manuscript can be improved and made more saleable. You will probably have to put up with substantial editing even if you are eventually lucky enough to secure a deal.

Importantly you would not submit your first draft to an agent or a publisher. The draft you send must be complete and as polished as you can make it.

If you are to achieve your ambition of becoming a published author, your draft manuscript must be distinctive, well written, well plotted, interesting, credible and the story must be about gripping characters. So, ensure that your story is complete and that it makes sense. Ensure it runs in a logical order. Of course, each writer works differently, so that some writers produce highly detailed plot summaries before they start writing while others make the story up as they go along. They are known in the trade as plotters or pantsers - flying by the seat of their pants.

If you produce a fully plotted plan, then the process of writing your novel is largely about fleshing out the structure that you have already created. However, if you begin with a looser structure, but edit and correct as you go, you can still end up with a relatively polished first draft.
Those who write more quickly without much of a plot outline while they produce a completed narrative, may well leave inconsistencies and gaps or sections that are not fully developed. The author will have to return to these once the first outline draft is complete.

These are all perfectly legitimate ways to write, but they do carry different implications in terms of how much revision you need to apply to the first draft. You need to be aware of how you write and take responsibility for the work you still require to do after the first draft is finished.

Chapter Seven

Producing a Polished Manuscript

However you write, you need to have your draft edited and it is important at this point to address the various issues dealt with in the previous chapter before you progress further. This means you must ensure you have a finished product. If you do not, there is no point approaching agents or publishers. Do not deceive yourself that your book is so brilliant, so original and so marketable that agents or publishers will overlook basic flaws. It is theoretically possible that they will, but it is more likely that the flaws will be the difference between a positive or negative response, or no response at all.

Agents and publishers are looking for talented writers, but they are also looking for that talent to be combined with discipline and commitment.

If they are to invest their time and their money in you as an author, they must be confident that you can write and deliver good quality work to a timescale. Authors must also be able to respond to editorial requests and suggestions, as well as being able to deal with the demands of the publication and production process. Then, if you are lucky, you will need to do the same again with all your subsequent books. This is to say, you will be required to be professional.

It is not possible for writers to get away with being unreliable and irresponsible. That does not mean you must act like a robot. However, agents and publishers will expect, indeed demand, a high standard of dedication, responsiveness and effort from you. Amongst the many aspiring authors, only a tiny proportion ever get to be published. Think about it, why should any agent or publisher spend their time or money on a writer who does not even get the basics right? The message is simple: before you even start to think about preparing your draft for submission - finish it.

Once that is done and you have filled in all the gaps, and the draft is finished to a standard that you are happy with, the next stage is one that many debut authors overlook. Give yourself the perspective of time and space and put your manuscript aside for a while. Do not decide to trust your own judgement, especially not immediately upon finishing the draft.

Once you have reached the end, you will either believe that in front of you is the finest work since *Jane Eyre* or *Oliver Twist* or that you have wasted your time writing a lot of rubbish. In reality, it is probably neither of these things, but you are not capable of judging your own work, especially when you have just finished writing the novel.

At this point, you will be very aware of the weaknesses in the story because there are always points when you struggle to make the plot work or where you were conscious of your lack of expertise. Also, you have been immersed in the story you have been writing. Only you know precisely who your characters are and what motivates them. You alone know their secrets. And because you know how the plot works, and how the different parts of the story lock into place around each other, details that may be obvious to you may not be at all clear to your reader.

Therefore, the received advice is to put your draft aside, probably for a few weeks. While this is difficult, it is worth doing. Take the time to write something else. Enter a competition, write a short story, go on a writing course or even start a second novel. When you come back to your draft, you have a much better chance of being objective. At this point you, will probably find that the book is both better and worse than you thought.

You will find the book is better because all the difficulties of writing it are now behind you. Now you can focus on how it actually reads. Of course, as you are no longer immersed in the story day after day, you will inevitably see its weaknesses including where clarification of the plot is needed and where the characters must be further developed or, where the points have been written in so much detail that it slows down the plot.

You need to identify an approach to editing which works best for you. Here you are not at the stage of producing a polished draft, but you do want to have all the basics in place.

Despite this, the first edit after you have picked up the completed draft again is a critical step in the writing process. This is when you are most likely to spot work that needs to be done to tidy up the plot, clarify the narrative and cut out unnecessary detail and description. It is amazing how many editing opportunities you can identify personally just by putting the draft aside and giving yourself a little perspective. When you are reviewing your own work, you must be ruthless about considering important issues that you need to address when reviewing your novel.

You should first consider the pace of the story. Make sure it does not drag. This can happen when, in early drafts there are passages that are inserted more to benefit the author than the readers. One example of this might be details of activities that the author inserts while they work out how a character gets from one place to another. There might also be descriptions of characters or their background that are used by the author while they decide the causes that make their characters act the way they do. Much plot development may be long winded and must be cut by the author after they have made sure that the story can be improved when they prune it. This discipline is necessary to give you, as the author, confidence that your novel makes sense, because, realistically, the details you cut are of little interest to the reader. They slow the story down.

Sometimes, however, the opposite is also true. If you have cut corners, you may need to add details to provide the reader with information they need to understand the story and the character dynamics properly. In these cases, you need to ensure that you revise the story and expand the parts needed to provide necessary description, scenic detail or development of any of your characters.

What you need to do is to ask yourself, while you are re-reading the novel, if you found the book gripping. Be brutal. Be aware of any sections where a reader might lose interest or skim over the writing rather than continue reading. Cut out the boring bits. You need to make sure that the pace of the story feels appropriate and that no sections are too slow or too rushed. Ask yourself if any part of the book feels unnecessarily repetitive. Alternatively, you must make sure you have not glossed over important details that would help the story hang together for the readers.

You also need to think about your characters. It does not matter whether they are likeable or unlikeable, good or evil, but they must be credible and interesting. Be honest with yourself. Do you find them engaging? Ask yourself if they are necessary to allow you to tell the story. If characters are uninteresting or do not add to the flow of the story, cut them out. Stephen King quoted author and Nobel prize winner William Faulkner, who said:

"In writing, you must kill all your darlings."

This literary advice refers to the danger of an author using their personal favourite elements of their story. While these may hold special meaning for the author, they may be of no interest to the readers. As an author, it is difficult to be dispassionate enough to decide which characters you find least interesting. It is harder still to decide which characters' reactions and motivations come across as realistic. You need to make it clear to the reader why the characters behaved as they did. To do this make sure your story contains sufficient information about each of the characters.

You also need to review the plot. It is important that it is easy to follow, and you may have to fix all the points that might confuse the reader. Alternatively, there may be parts of the plot that require extra explanation or clarification. Equally, consider whether any plot details are laboured or more detailed than they need to be. You also must be sensitive to points of the plot where it does not work or make sense. If this is the case, you must rework them diligently.

On re-reading the book you must make sure that the story is believable. You have to be sure that there are no points in your story that are incredible or unconvincing. This must be genre specific because expectations of a fantasy or science fiction book, for example, will be different from those of a crime novel. In any event, the narrative must work. If there are any parts of the book where your lack of knowledge or level of research are evident, re-write those paragraphs.

Lastly, the locations and settings must feel interesting and well described. They must be convincing to the reader. Make sure there are no points where the reader needs a more or, indeed, less detailed description.

When you answer these questions honestly, it will help you to identify the areas where there is scope to improve or refine your book.

Chapter Eight

Produce a Chapter Plan and First Draft Synopsis

This is one of the most difficult but worthwhile tasks you should complete at this stage. It is to write a first draft of a short synopsis of your book. This is likely to be particularly useful if you do not work from a detailed outline plan and even if you do, this is a good point to step back and confirm that the story you have written matches your outline.

Writing a draft synopsis at this stage is useful for many reasons. Most obviously, because you will need to prepare one at some point as all agents and publishers will expect a synopsis as part of your submission. If you produce a first draft at this stage, you can continue to refine it as you develop and polish your overall manuscript. You can also adapt it depending on the length and style of synopsis a particular agent or publisher demands. In effect, it will provide you with a foundation document which you can condense and adapt to support your submissions.

Also, the discipline of preparing a summary of your book will help you identify any specific errors in the plot or structure. It is much easier to sort problems within the plot or timeline if you reduce a novel to a few hundred words. A useful way of doing this is to reduce each chapter to the size of an original tweet - 140 characters to a maximum of 2,000 words in total. You must focus only on summarising your narrative in the order it appears. Summarising in this way will help you assess the coherence and balance of your novel. The word count should be long enough to enable you to capture the main events of your story but also force you to consider what must be excluded.

Consider the decisions you have made on what to exclude from the synopsis because these decisions may prompt questions about whether these parts of the book should be included in the novel at all. If you decide to exclude a sub-plot or scene from the synopsis, consider whether you need it.

Of course, there are many reasons for including a scene apart from advancing the plot. A scene may be needed to provide insight into a character's reaction or their motivation. Alternatively, it may be needed to establish atmosphere. But, particularly in commercial fiction, scenes which do not contribute to the plot should be few and far between. If a sub-plot does not contribute to the central narrative, its value is always going to be questionable. If you find it difficult to describe the links between the main story and a sub-plot, you may wish to consider whether the structure of your novel requires changing or perhaps the sub-plot should be deleted.

Equally, if you find yourself struggling to explain concisely how the different elements of the narrative fit together, you may want to consider whether the overall story actually works or if it is too complicated.

If you are preparing your chapter tweet sized notes and find you are struggling to summarise the book this way, perhaps in terms of sub-plots or timelines, you may deduce that you should simplify your story.

Even if this summary is longer than most agents or publishers require, it is a good starting point. You may also find this will be a valuable reference document because you can use this chapter summary as the basis for developing a synopsis of the book to be sent to agents or publishers when you reach that stage.

You will find that synopses requirements of agents and publishers vary widely; the only common thread is that they are looking for quite a short document. This is often no more than a few paragraphs on one side of A4 making it a total of about 500 words.

Basically, any synopsis that you send to an agent or a publisher is, in reality, a sales pitch and a summary of your book.

Chapter Nine

The Value of Beta Readers

Once your first edit is done, you are likely to find it helpful, but daunting, to seek the opinions of others. It is a brave step. You may be reluctant to let anyone read what you have written until you have completed a draft that you are happy with. Alternatively, you may prefer to allow trusted readers to read sections of your book as you write. Do whatever is most comfortable to you.

Nevertheless, this is important, and it is definitely worthwhile seeking the opinions of others. Many established writers have built up networks of these trusted critics or *beta readers*. They are given first sight of a draft book and asked to give feedback. These readers are invaluable in identifying both strengths and weaknesses in the draft that are often not obvious to the author.

Building a reliable panel of beta readers takes time, therefore it is worth identifying potential people whenever you have something for them to read. Think about the kind of beta readers you need. The last of these points is probably the most important. The only purpose of submitting your novel to others is to obtain *honest* feedback on your book. To this end, do not select beta readers who will be reluctant to offend you or say anything critical about your work. It is better to avoid approaching very close friends or family members. Other authors, writing group members or book bloggers, although busy, make excellent beta readers.

Bear in mind that when you ask for an honest opinion, you have to be willing to accept that not everyone will like all that you have written and may criticise some of your favourite scenes or question your use of particular characters. This hurts. It is like being told you have an ugly baby and you must be thick skinned about it.

Indeed, if you ask someone to read your book as a beta reader, do tell them that you *want* their views. You must make it clear that you will not be offended by what they have to say. You have to stick by this and not show disappointment if you receive critical feedback. Also, try not to be too pushy or send out your draft unsolicited. Asking someone to read a draft manuscript is a huge commitment, and many people whose views you would appreciate may not have time to take on that job. Others may not want to put themselves in a position where they have to criticise or offer a negative opinion on aspects of your draft.

If someone does accept a request to beta read for you, explain that the feedback does not have to be lengthy or detailed, but should reflect their views honestly. Having said that, it is always useful to find one or two beta readers who are prepared to give you thorough comments on a chapter by chapter basis.

It may be helpful to the beta readers, especially if they are inexperienced, if you provide prompt questions, for example:

- Did you find the book entertaining? Were there any sections where you lost interest or struggled to continue reading? Were there any parts where the story felt unclear or rushed?
- Did you find the characters engaging? Which characters interested you most? Did you know enough (or too much) about each character?
- Did you find the plot easy to follow? Were there any points where you found yourself confused? Were there any points where you felt the plot did not make sense?
- Did you find the book credible? Were there points where the story felt far-fetched or unconvincing?

- Did you find the book's setting interesting? Were there any points where you would have liked more, or less, description about the setting?
- What other books did this novel remind you of? How do you feel it compared with them?

If beta readers are asked to respond to specific questions, it is easier for them to give you the balanced feedback you need. It also means they will feel less awkward about offering a negative point of view if they feel this is offset with a positive comment relating to other aspects of the novel.

You must accept the feedback, positive and negative, with a good grace. You may disagree with some of it, you may ignore most of it, but when it represents an honest opinion from someone who is trying to help you, be humble.

Even if you disagree with the feedback, think about why this reader feels that way. If the reader indicates that they perceived a plot hole, even if you think the plot makes sense, consider that part of the story again and think why the reader was left with that impression. It may be that you have failed to describe the developments as clearly as you thought you had; you may need to expand the narrative a little just to make the story line more obvious. If the reader feels the pace is too slow or too hurried, you might not agree but, again, consider if you can improve the story at that point to avoid other readers feeling that way.

Of course, you can never please every reader and you should not try to do so. Everybody has different tastes, and you will receive feedback that you decide to disregard. You will also probably get contradictory feedback from different beta readers. Still, even if you decide that the feedback is unjustified or does not reflect the story you are trying to tell, it should give you something to think about.

If you get to a stage where you use a regular panel of beta readers, you will become more familiar with their preferences. You will learn which ones have views closest to yours, and those with which you tend to disagree. You will discover which beta readers take time to give you detailed feedback and those who provide a brief overview. Ideally, you should build up a diverse panel who will provide you with a broad range of feedback and challenge your thinking and assumptions.

Using beta readers to help improve that first finished draft, is invaluable at this stage, especially for a debut or inexperienced author. But there is nothing to prevent you seeking the views of beta readers at a later stage too. Their observations can be very helpful even as late as at the final step before submission. This can help you produce a polished, final version of your novel. At that time, you are likely to need more detailed feedback about the content or structure of the book. This may lead you to select readers prepared to respond at greater length.

Chapter Ten

The Importance of Being Edited

You want to edit your work to produce a final draft that is as polished as you can make it prior to submission. Understand, however, that as much work as you do on the manuscript at this stage, it will only be the start of the editing process.

If you are fortunate enough to be accepted by an agent or publisher, they will have their own views about how the book can be further improved. You may not agree with all of their suggestions, but, like your beta readers, remember that they are trying to help you improve your novel. The book will be subject to an even more detailed editorial process prior to publication.

Authors often find this process frustrating, especially when you may feel as if you are not making progress. Remember though, this is a critical part of improving your work and making it more saleable. When you have worked your way through the differences of opinion, you will almost always end up with a far better book. Having said that, many authors hate the editing process. It feels less creative than the writing process, and, depending on the state of your initial manuscript, can be a challenging time. Sometimes you may feel that while you sort a hole in the plot or a timing issue, all you do is add many more problems. It is hard work and it requires concentration and attention to detail. Having said that, it is necessary to present your work in the best possible light.

The first question you need to consider is how much you want to edit your manuscript before submitting it to an agent or publisher. Many writers worry that, if they send out a draft that is too polished, agents and publishers may not see any potential for developing or changing the book to meet their stable or imprint. While there may be a little truth in this, an agent or publisher will definitely look for potential before they seek a perfectly polished piece.

However, there is far more danger that, in working through a large pile of submissions, an agent or publisher will be distracted by superficial problems with your draft and therefore fail to see its best qualities. Should your draft suffer from repetition, too much description, or unrealistic dialogue, an agent or publisher may decide not to read further and thus fail to appreciate the strength of your novel.

Edit your manuscript until you are really pleased with it. If you are not happy with it, you should not want to show it to anybody else. It is largely a matter of self-esteem and self-confidence. If you have any doubt about the quality of your book or if you are aware of flaws that you could have fixed, then you will not do your submission justice. Your covering letter will not have the intrinsic enthusiasm to pique the interest of an agent or publisher.

More and more debut authors decide to have their work professionally edited prior to submitting their novel to an agent or publisher. This is not cheap, but it is certainly worth considering if you can afford to do it.

You must first identify a reputable editor. The services editors offer vary widely. Make sure the type of edit you secure is actually what you are looking for. Services range from a review or critique of your manuscript all the way to a detailed structural edit or even copy-editing.

If you find a high-quality editor, you can be confident that your book has been reviewed by an experienced professional who is independent and objective. They should have a good knowledge of the publishing world and standards that will be expected of you. However, as with the feedback from your beta readers, you must be prepared to receive and accept negative comments.

There are downsides to having your draft professionally edited. The first and most obvious of these is that it does cost money. The amount you pay will vary according to the editor you choose and on the scope of the services you request. The length of your manuscript will also be relevant as will the amount of work that the editor needs to do. A full-scale structural and copy edit is likely to command a much higher price tag than a more cursory review.

The other potential downside is that you must secure the appropriate editor. You must make sure that the editor you choose is not only well-qualified but experienced in editing the type of book you have written. Therefore, you must find an editor who is not just used to working in your genre but also with a good knowledge of what agents and publishers are looking for. You may have contacts who can recommend an editor, but you may also be wise to check with the relevant professional bodies. In the UK the best place to look for an editor is by contacting the Society of Editors and Proof-readers www.sfep.org.uk. It is certainly worthwhile to have your manuscript professionally edited if you can afford it. However, you may feel you can review and revise your draft to a good standard without investing in that professional editorial support.

It is probably useful at this point to consider the main types and levels of editing that are available for your book.

The many terms that are used by editors, whether you employ one privately or have one assigned to you by your publisher, can be confusing to a debut author. Of course, it is unhelpful that the distinctions between the different types of edit are not obvious. They unavoidably overlap.

Let us consider the main types of edit available. You may want a developmental or structural edit, a copy-edit or you might instruct you editor to proofread your work.

Developmental or structural editing is the most fundamental level of editing. If you ask the editor for this level of revision, you should expect them to review the whole structure of your novel as well as the plot. The editor will also comment on the development of your characters, and the ways you have dealt with the themes of your novel. However, it is not unknown for some publishers to draw a distinction between developmental and structural editing. When they do this, they normally use the developmental edit to mean a review of the constituent parts of the book, while they consider a structural edit to refer to the way the book is organised. The editor will draw to your attention the issues they identify. This distinction is more likely to be made in relation to non-fiction books. You can consider the developmental and structural edit as the same thing when dealing with a work of fiction. To summarise, this level of editing is intended to improve the overall structure and presentation of your story.

The second type of editing mentioned above was copy editing. This involves a more detailed, line by line review of your novel. You can expect the editor to consider issues that should include ensuring continuity with regard to your descriptions. If necessary, they will also advise on improving the clarity of the language you have used. They will also remove repetitive and redundant language.

For debut authors looking to submit their work to agents or publishers, this is probably the most critical level of editing. Any agent or publisher will usually make a decision on whether to take your submission further on little more than a brief read through of the extract you submit. If the language seems clumsy or unclear, they will most likely move it to the *reject* pile no matter how good your idea or plot.

Of course, the quality of your book requires to be excellent too. But getting your book published requires you to overcome a series of hurdles. This is the first of those and it is without doubt the most challenging.

You are just a name in a letter or on an e-mail and your name is one amongst thousands. At this point, you have only one chance to grab the attention of that agent or publisher, so you must do everything you can to get it. Securing that first interest is critical. Once you have done that and you have secured a degree of interest in your work, they will be more than willing to help you make your manuscript fit for publication. You will find that the level of help and support the agent or publisher will make available to you increases at each stage as their commitment to your work grows. But the process never becomes easy. Even as an established author, you must work hard to sustain the quality of your work.

So, for any author, but particularly a debut author, a good copy-edit is vital. If you only have a limited amount of money to invest in your draft and want to secure professional editing advice, this is the edit to choose. But if you cannot afford a professional editor, you can do a great deal yourself with careful revision and objective consideration of your writing.

The final level of editing is proofreading. This is the most detailed level of all the edits. It is most concerned with spotting spelling errors, typing mistakes and grammatical issues that were not noticed during the copy-edit. As such, proofreading sounds straightforward, but it demands a great deal of skill and concentration. It also requires a good knowledge of spelling and grammar.

Everybody tends to read what they expect to be on the page as opposed to what is there. This makes it especially difficult to proofread your own work. You are much too close to it. You know what you meant to say, and you are unlikely to notice that you wrote something different. Bearing that in mind you need to make sure that your manuscript has been properly proofread. If you can afford to have to it professionally proofread, then do that. If not, it is worth finding one or two beta readers with good spelling and grammar skills and ask them to read and review your draft carefully with those aspects in mind.

No agent or publisher will reject your submission because it contains one or two spelling errors. However, if your spelling or grammar is consistently poor, they are much less likely to read your work further.

If you cannot afford a professional editor to advise you about your work and, if, like most of us, you do not know an editor who is prepared to work for free, then the only option is to edit it as well as you can yourself. It is particularly bad form to approach an editor you know and put pressure on them to work on your novel for free. That is what they do for a living. It is how they pay their bills. They may offer *mates' rates*, but do not expect them to complete a professional edit of a full-length novel at no charge. You will embarrass them and yourself.

It is very hard to edit your own manuscript. You have put a great deal of time, energy and emotional commitment into the draft. No doubt you know why you wrote the book in the way you did and exactly what you were trying to achieve in each scene. So, if you already think your book is as good as you can make it, it is particularly difficult to change anything at all. This is a huge emotional hurdle.

Even if your book is excellent, and it must be very good to stand any hope of being accepted by an agent or publisher, it will not be perfect at this stage. There will be plenty of ways to improve it and maximise your chances of having it accepted. That is not meant as a criticism of your skills as a writer. It is a simple truth. Even experienced and well-known authors produce drafts that need to be edited, perhaps even substantially edited, before their work is fit for publication.

Often authors feel their hearts sink when they get editorial feedback. But they do come to love their editors because they know they help to make the very best of the stories they create. You must be as honest with yourself as you can and before you proceed further stop and challenge yourself with regard to every scene and each character. If they are superlative and do not add anything useful to the narrative, *kill your darlings*!

For example, if your plot twist is overly clever or unexpected, it may be completely incredible or perhaps you have failed to explain the necessary mechanics that make it work properly. Equally, if you are particularly fond of one of your characters, it is difficult to be aware that you have not described the character fully to the reader. Do try to be systematic in how you approach the draft at this stage, rather than fiddling with it in a piecemeal way.

First, focus on the overall structure of your draft. Then proceed to review your book with increasing attention to detail. Try not to be tempted to play about with other details while you are working on the structure. This means you will be less likely to introduce further problems as you edit. For example, if you make a change to the structure of your novel, you may subsequently need to amend the way you introduce some characters or share information with the reader. If you approach these points in an orderly fashion, you will reduce the risk of continuity errors, timing problems and other issues.

Chapter Eleven

Review the Structure of Your Book

When you are reviewing the structure of your book, you may find it helpful to return to the chapter summary which you produced.

Chapter	Setting
If your chapters comprise more than one scene, produce a summary for each scene. This will identify chapters that are too long or complicated.	Depending on the genre, this might include geographical setting, featured locations and the date or time. The last of these can be particularly valuable if the story involves multiple timelines or if you need to ensure that parallel events occur in sequence.
	Featured Characters
	List the characters appearing in the chapter. This is especially useful if the presence or absence of a character in a scene is important.
	If you have not already produced a list of your characters and their physical appearance and personal qualities, you may also find it helpful to add details about background, motivations and attitudes as they occur in the narrative. This ensures consistency.

	Summary of Events
	Finally, summarise in no more than a few sentences the main events of the chapter. Identify who does or says what and what happens.
	Sub-Plots and Narrative Strand
	If your novel contains multiple sub-plots or narrative strands, give each of these a title or label and note here to which strand the chapter or scene contributes.
	This will help you track the balance and relationship between the various strands as the story progresses. It might be that some of the stands link together, and you can note all the relevant strands here and highlight the links.

The last heading here will probably be the most useful in helping you to review the structure of your book. The use of colour coding might help give a clearer perspective on the overall shape of the book too. This might show whether any of the strands or sub-plots appear out of balance with the rest of the story, or if the narrative shifts appropriately between the various threads.

There are no right or wrong answers here. Some very successful novels follow a highly linear narrative with only limited sub-plots. Others combine multiple narrative strands, sub-plots and timeframes, moving fluidly between them. Again, some devote discrete sections of the narrative to each. Only you can determine the structure and arrangement that works best for your novel. The more conscious you are of the shape of your book, and of the structural choices available, the more you will shape your book in a way that ensures the story is told as effectively as possible.

If the feedback on your work indicates that the pace of the book drags a bit, or if your beta readers found the story less than gripping, then you need to consider whether the structure supports or impedes your narrative. There may be reasons as to why the story in your book feels slow and these can often be addressed at the copyediting stage. However, if the overall structure simply doesn't work, all other problems are distinctly secondary.

The most common structural problem, for inexperienced writers, is that the plot is too complicated. This is usually because they have included too many themes, narrative strands or even sub-plots. If you re-read your book and find that this may be the case, try to summarise the main narrative strands or sub-plots. Do this thoroughly and list each theme, plot or sub-plot, narrative strand and character in order of their importance to the novel. Put the most important first. Once you have done this, you are in a good position to streamline the story or cut any characters that are surplus to requirements.

Really, unless you are aiming to write a very lengthy epic or saga, and this would be ambitious for a debut author, you would not normally have more than three or four main characters, narrative strands or sub-plots. Likewise, if you try to weave in more than that, many readers will struggle to follow your story or to remember which character is which. So, if your novel is more complicated than that, re-read with an uncompromising eye and think how many of them are truly necessary or whether some could be cut or reduced. Remember, you must be brave if you need to be and kill your darlings.

Bear in mind also, that your readers expect each strand or sub-plot to contribute to the story in the book. This does not mean that each stand must tie up neatly at the end, but it does mean that every strand must merit its place. If you found it difficult to define the purpose of any strand or sub-plot or character, you should seriously think whether it should be cut without out adversely affecting your novel.

Narrative strands and sub-plots can be very useful. Often, authors use them to reveal the story from a variety of perspectives.

In crime fiction, for example, the story might involve several murders or crimes that appear to be unconnected, then the links are revealed to expose the murderer and their motives. If any strand does not contribute to the overall plot, be sure that it contributes in a different other way. For example, it may provide contrast to the main plot in terms of tone, humour or atmosphere.

The benefit of using multiple plot strands is that they allow the author an easy way to vary the pace in the story. In terms of readability, the author can also build tension or suspense and intrigue by introducing new characters, priorities or settings.

It is possible to leave one plot strand on a cliff-hanger and keep the reader in suspense, waiting for a resolution, by moving to a different plot line, or by moving from a fast-paced scene to one that is slower and more reflective. It is perfectly possible to tell a gripping story in a linear way but if an author uses parallel plots it provides them with an additional way of holding the reader's attention. However, if there are too many narrative strands or plot lines and characters and the story cuts between them too radically, the reader may feel confused or unable to engage with each narrative or character because the story moves too fast from one narrative to the next. Consider whether any strand is redundant or does not link to the main story, if this is the case, resolve the issue because, if you do not, the reader is likely to be dissatisfied.

If you have colour coded your chapter summary it may help you review the sequencing and interaction of your various narrative strands speedily. If you notice that you stick with one particular narrative strand for several chapters before moving on, consider whether the pace of the book would be improved by changing the order of some scenes or chapters in a way that the story moves more readily between the various plot lines.

Of course, if you find that the story in your novel moves between different strands on a chapter by chapter basis, it may be that the reader will find the pace is too confusing or frenetic. It may be that you will find the pace is improved by moving chapters about or clustering some of the scenes together. Judge the structure that is best for your novel.

A scene that might seem overly long or misplaced may make sense just the way it is if, for example, it builds suspense before a dramatic event that has been foreshadowed to the reader.

Cuts between parallel events are often very effective if you want to show that the pace of the story is accelerating. However, slower scenes may work well when you want to slow down the pace in your novel to allow the reader to think about things that have just happened or to prepare them for incidents to come.

When you have finished considering how to balance the multiple storylines, narrative strands, sub-plots and characters, you should also consider whether your story is written in the best order possible. Think about this carefully because even if the core narrative is straightforward, the impact it makes on the reader may be increased by beginning with a dramatic event. You may decide initially to withhold relevant information from the reader, and then gradually reveal the sequence of events that led up to that point.

In crime fiction, for example, books often commence with the discovery of the crime. The subsequent investigation then uncovers how and why the crime was committed, ending with the reader discovering who the culprit is. The result of this is that *whodunit* crime fiction, often requires to balance at least two parallel narratives. These are the progress of the investigation and the earlier happenings that caused the commission of the crime.

Whatever genre your book falls into, start your story with a scene that will grab the attention of the reader and draw them into your narrative. To do this you want to plunge them right into the centre of the action. This is so that they want to read on to find out more about your characters, why and how the situation came to be, and crucially, what happens next. You need them to read on but if you start your book with a long chapter that gradually introduces the characters, tells the reader all about their life and backstory, and only then goes on to a description of the dramatic events, it is likely that you will have lost the reader's interest and they will never make it to the dramatic events.

You want the reader to read and enjoy your book. With this in mind, it is worth thinking carefully about whether your story starts in the right place. This is especially important for an inexperienced novelist looking to be published. You will have only one opportunity to grab the attention of any agent or publisher. Therefore, make your opening scene as effective as possible. Read it again and consider whether it is the best one to make them want to read on.

Bear in mind that the most effective opening scene may not be the most clearly dramatic. Indeed, it may make more impact if you avoid an opening which might be seen as predictable. Although crime novels do often begin with the discovery of a dead body or perhaps with someone being followed before being attacked. These scenes are certainly dramatic, but an experienced agent or publisher may feel that it is not original enough to catch their interest.

You may be able to address this by ensuring that the scene is distinctive, or you can address the issue by opening the novel in an intriguing place. It is also worth considering whether the first scene reflects the overall feel of your book. If your novel is character-driven, then it is sensible to ensure that readers are able to engage with your characters right from the start. However, if the story is plot-driven or action-oriented, then it will be more effective to begin with a dramatic event.

To consider whether your story begins at the right point, both to engage the reader and to establish the overall tone of your work, you may find it useful to think about these questions in relation to your opening scene.

* Does it reflect the feel and tone of the book overall?
* Does it engage the reader and make them want to read on?
* Are significant characters introduced? If so, does it tell readers enough about them, and make the reader want to know more? If not, does this matter, and does the scene give the reader another reason to carry on reading?

If you are struggling to think of an answer to these questions, it might be that you should identify a more effective opening to your book. You may find that you have an existing scene that you can move, or you might be better to write a new scene that dramatises an event referenced later. Either way, you should identify a suitable scene or chapter, and think about how that would relate to the questions above. It may be sensible to deconstruct the scene with these issues in mind.

Chapter Twelve

Characters and Points of View

After you have considered the overall structure of your novel, there are other issues that should be considered during your structural review of the book.

These include the number and diversity of characters and the point, or points, of view that you use. In this regard, first consider your novel as a whole.

Look at your chapter summary. Here you have already listed all the characters in your book, along with their brief descriptions. One of the most important issues you must address, especially if the beta readers found parts of the book dragged or not very interesting, is whether you need all the characters.

It might be that if some of the characters are deleted or combined you could cut out or shorten some scenes without adversely affecting the overall structure of your novel. By removing a character that only appears in a few scenes and reallocating the small plot contribution they make to other characters, you should be able to remove some unnecessary scenes and simplify others. This should make the story flow at a more acceptable pace to the reader and while there is no definite right way of doing this, you must find the balance that is best for your story.

If your novel only has a small number of characters, you must ensure that they are sufficiently interesting to carry the story and sustain the reader's interest all the way through the book. However, should you have a large number of characters, you must ensure that they are memorable, and that the reader does not need to keep checking which character is which.

To make sure the book is as good as it can be, check your list of characters and, with regard to each of them, ask the following questions:

* Why is the character in the novel?
* What role do they play, and how do they drive the story forward?
* Is the character distinctive?
* Would it be detrimental to the story if you removed them?

Another very crucial issue is the use of point of view in your book. Point of view is often an issue that debut novelists find particularly difficult, and it is not uncommon for an inexperienced writer to jump between several different points of view throughout the book and sometimes even within one scene. If point of view is not properly handled, readers may find it not only distracting but also confusing. This will make the book harder for them to read with enjoyment.
You will want to look at the way you handle point of view in detail in individual scenes at a later point but just now, consider how you tell the story as a whole.

A story told in the first person must, by definition, stick firmly to a single point of view. In these novels everything is related from the point of view of the character who is the narrator. This keeps the point of view simple and is a useful device in some kinds of fiction.

For example, it is commonly used in psychological thrillers or detective novels where the author only wants the reader to know as much as the narrator. This means that important information can be justifiably withheld until it is revealed to the narrator in the story.

This can be most effective, but it imposes considerable constraints on the author. If the whole story is told in the first person, the writer has no obvious way to reveal information to the reader which the narrator does not yet know. However, a writer can probably find ways of providing the narrator with key information without the character realising its significance. This can be a lot of fun and is often a most effective narrative device. However, you should be aware that, the reader may feel cheated if a first-person narrator withholds something relevant about themselves without good reason. This is an instance of *the unreliable narrator.* It is often possible to establish a plausible reason to justify the narrator's unreliability. So, although first person narration can be very effective, it often constrains the author's ability to present a complicated story.

Many writers prefer to narrate their story in the third person. This can be done either using an omniscient narrator or, more commonly in contemporary novels, from the perspective of one or more of the key characters in the book. An omniscient narrator can tell the reader the actions and thoughts of all characters in the book. Using the point of view of several characters gives the author a freedom that first person point of view does not.

If your novel is written in the third person, try to keep the number of points of view quite small. Normally, the story would be told primarily from the outlook of the main protagonist but using other viewpoints in scenes where the main protagonist does not appear. In these scenes, you may want to consider keeping the points of view as consistent as possible across the book so that a given narrative strand is always told from the same outlook unless there is a practical reason why this is not possible. But there are no absolute rules.

There may be a good reason to narrate a scene from a different perspective as this might provide the reader with new insights into the story. Equally, you may want to hold back information about what a character thinks or feels about a piece of action and therefore you decide to narrate the scene from another character's point of view. Alternatively, you may want to change things about and if you stay with the outlooks of just one or two characters throughout the whole book the reader may begin to feel almost claustrophobic. Only you can decide what works for your book. Just bear in mind that, if the point of view shifts too often or if your story has too many viewpoints, the reader may be distracted or confused.

If your book is written in the third person, it would be sensible at this point to go through your chapter plan and note, for each chapter or scene, the viewpoint from which the story is told. Add this information into your chapter summary. In order to do this, you must ask yourself:

* Is the point of view clear in each scene or chapter?
To check if the point of view changes, read the scene back to yourself as if it were written in the first person. If the first-person character changes, you have a point of view issue that needs to be fixed.

* Make a note of how many viewpoints you use across the book?
If you are using a several, review those that recur least often and think about whether there is a justification for using them, or whether you can reduce the overall number of outlooks.

* How often does the point of view switch between chapters?
Even a small number of different viewpoints, if changed frequently, may be confusing or distracting to the reader.

* Is the story told largely from a small number of points of view?
If most of your story is told from only one or two outlooks, consider whether you need the other points of view. It may be that you do, but just ask yourself whether the additional points of view contribute positively to the telling of the story.

Of course, there are some instances where writers use a mixture of first and third person to tell their story. This can be a most effective technique if you want to tell some parts of the story from a particularly restricted point of view but want to exercise greater freedom in other chapters of the book. Some readers like this, but it must be skilfully handled, otherwise it can be distracting and a bit gimmicky. If you choose to use a less conventional technique like this, be completely certain that it is appropriate and effective in the context of the story.

Also consider the consistency of points of view. Editors normally advise that you stick with the same point of view throughout each individual scene, and that you do not *head hop* between your characters. While this is not a hard and fast rule and it is possible to shift between viewpoints within a scene, it does need to be handled very skilfully otherwise but it can distract the reader.

Think about it, if the reader sit inside one character's head, they can empathise with that character. This becomes much harder for the reader if they are asked to shift perspectives. It is likely that the reader will become more detached from the scene. This is why one viewpoint for each scene is preferable. So, if your book is written in the third person, review the point of view in the opening scene or chapter. Consider if the point of view you have chosen is the most appropriate one and also whether there would be a positive or negative impact if you changed that viewpoint to another character. Also check that you have been consistent in your use of point of view.

Now you have revised the whole of your first scene or chapter by applying all the principles discussed so far. It should now be as polished as you can make it. This means it will have the best chance of making a positive impact when submitted to an agent or publisher.

Chapter Thirteen

Copyedit Your Own Book

You have, by now, looked at the steps needed to ensure that the structure of your book is sound and tells your story the way you want it to be told. You should also have finished the structural changes you found that were needed.

To be honest, you may feel that you have taken a step backwards. In fact, depending on the amount of change you decided to make, you probably feel that you have torn your nice neat manuscript apart and that all you have left are ragged edges. It may even be true, but you really have made substantial progress in making sure that your submission will be as good as it can be. So now you must improve your manuscript on a page by page, line by line basis. Of course, that will include sorting out all those ragged edges. This is the process of copyediting.

Copyediting is the process of making your writing as good as you can make it in terms of its impact, clarity and readability. Be aware that effective copyediting is an appreciable skill and, therefore, if you can afford it, it is worthwhile having your novel professionally copyedited before you submit it to an agent or publisher. If you are not able to pay a copyeditor, it is worth polishing and refining your work as far as you can before submission. There are some steps you can learn to help you do that for yourself.

You must work through your manuscript chapter by chapter, working on each scene, paragraph and sentence to make sure they are as effective as possible. There are no hard and fast rules about how to edit your work, or about what style of writing is best. Bear in mind, successful writing can be as sparse as Ernest Hemingway's or as ornate as Charles Dickens's. You must decide what works in your manuscript and for the story you want to tell. Nevertheless, there are some guidelines that you can apply to improve your work.

Begin with your first chapter and work through it to see if you can improve it. Generally speaking, you will find it easier to work through your novel from beginning to end. This is partly because at this point you will find it easier to spot any continuity errors, but you may also come across plot glitches that you might have introduced as a result of your structural edit.

It may be helpful when you are reviewing your work at this stage, to reread the feedback from your beta readers. Identify any of their comments that relate to the details in your writing. If any of the beta readers are good at commenting on your writing, it might be worth asking them to review your opening chapter more closely again and consider their additional comments.

Each author writes differently. If your first draft is underwritten and a bit too sketchy in relation to events, settings or characters to allow the reader to follow your story easily, then take time now to flesh out the details as needed. Because many authors strive to get down the story even if it is the bare bones of the story in the first place. This allows them to complete the shape of their story before filling out the characters, settings or even the exact details of the plot. This does not mean you have to provide overly ornate description. An economic style that can encourage readers to use their imagination is often most effective. However, the author must paint enough of a picture to allow the reader to colour in the picture for themselves. This can be done by providing a few details which set the scene or give an insight into one of the story's characters.

If your beta readers feel that your characters are two-dimensional, your story is difficult to follow or your settings unclear, you must find ways of adding detail.

There are several ways to do this apart from just adding detailed description. You can show your characters through descriptions of their behaviour or with dialogue. You can reveal details of the characters' appearance or explain a location through a mixture of narrative description and commentary between the characters. Of course, you can extend or add scenes to flesh out the narrative, as opposed to just recounting events. Good writing deploys a mixture of all of these techniques. So, ring the changes between them and this will allow the reader to enjoy your novel without noticing how they have come to understand the character or see the setting clearly.

Equally, you may overwrite in the first instance. Some authors describe this as writing their first draft for themselves and the second draft for the reader. What this means is that the first draft tends to include extended descriptions of characters and their backstories, of locations and of physical movements around a scene. The author may write these to ensure that they understand the character or situation but when they edit the first draft, they edit out the details the reader does not need to know, or that they can fill in from their own imagination. To leave these details in may slow down the narrative.

In the first edit, you may find that you can take out about a fifth of the words in your book without losing any substantial content. This may be some of the extra details but also some redundant words, unnecessary dialogue tags, adverbs or intensifiers that are not needed.

As you think about this, edit the first paragraph of your manuscript again. Remove anything that you feel adds little to the meaning. You may well find that you reduce the number of words but are able to add additional information that is useful to the reader. It is worth reviewing your use of adjectives, adverbs and adverb intensifiers. They all have a place in effective writing, but it can be easy to overuse them. Remove them and see if their absence makes a big difference to the meaning. Often, they add little that cannot easily be drawn from the context.

Now, take the first page of your novel and go through it word by word. Remove anything that adds nothing to the meaning or is a detail that the reader does not need at this point. Also, add any extra details that are needed to improve the reader's understanding. If you have been unable to remove any word, then it may be that you are a concise writer. Of course, it may be that you have not yet been strict enough with regard to your work.

Chapter Fourteen

Reading Out Loud

While you are copyediting your work by cutting or expanding it, you should also be aware of how it sounds. It can be worthwhile to read the manuscript out loud or even to record your reading of passages and play it back to yourself. In order to check that it is easy to read and to follow. If you find a sentence or phrase difficult to read out or if you find yourself stumbling over the wording, it might mean that the phrasing is clumsy or unclear. Similarly, as you read out loud, you will notice repetition in words or phrasing that may not be evident when you read the words on paper.

If a reader will have to stop to unravel your language to work out what is meant, change it to make it clear. Revise language that is repetitive or awkward. It is not easy to notice these faults in your own work because you know what you intended to say. It may be hard to admit that you are not saying it clearly.

When you have edited the first page of your novel, read it out loud and see if you spot any remaining repetition. If you did not find it easy to read, or if any of the phrasing felt awkward, then see what further changes you need to make to improve the book. The detailed work on your first page will provide you with a template to review the rest of the book. Yes, that will take a long time, but it is worth doing.

Chapter Fifteen

Dialogue Tags

Another area to check carefully is your use of dialogue tags. Inexperienced writers tend both to over-use '*he/she said*' and over-use variants such as '*he shouted*', '*she whispered*' and so on. It is amazing how often you are able to cut these tags without losing clarity about which character is speaking. Often, it is clear from the context who is saying what. Otherwise, you might be able to replace '*he/she said*' with a description of a related action that shows which character has spoken. For example, you could replace:

'I'm leaving,' he said, turning away.

with

'I'm leaving.' He turned away.

If you use these kinds of actions to replace dialogue tags you must be careful and make sure they are not too repetitive. It is easy to ·fall into the trap of having your characters always rubbing their nose, grinning or walking out of the door. However, if you use them carefully the use of these actions can make the dialogue feel more dynamic and help you avoid the repetition that occurs with the habitual use of '*he said*'. Trying to avoid this repetition often leads debut authors to overuse other phrases, including '*he exclaimed,*' or '*she muttered*'.

Your editor may recommend removing these phrases entirely, but there may be times where the use of them is justified. However, you may want to keep them to a minimum as their frequent use can be distracting to the reader.

This advice also holds good in respect of adverbs in dialogue tags. The tone of voice or emotions of the character should be clear from the context and from the dialogue itself. On this basis, you should not normally have to use phrases like *'he said angrily'* or *'she said calmly'*. If the meaning is unclear when you remove the adverb, think about whether your dialogue is clear enough.

Consider also that it is possible to remove too many dialogue tags because, if you have long sections of dialogue, you must make it easy for the reader to tell who is speaking. This is usually evident from the context, but it can be less obvious when multiple speakers are involved. If characters in a discussion are on the same side or are all contributing to a collective topic, perhaps such as police officers sharing information about a crime, dialogue tags may be necessary. However, even if there are only two characters involved and the dialogue alternates, you may still want to use occasional dialogue tags because it should not be necessary for the reader to have to count back through the discussion to work out who is speaking. If the section of speech is lengthy, consider adding in occasional dialogue indicators to make the speaker clear to the reader. For variety, sometimes these can be descriptions of actions rather than simply *'he said'*.

Now take a passage in your first chapter, or the first chapter in your book that contains speech and edit it with dialogue tags in mind. Think carefully about how you present the dialogue. Consider if you are slowing down the pace or if there is too much repetition with too much *'he said/she said'*. Also, if you have used alternative verbs, like "he muttered" or "she exclaimed", think about whether they add anything. Equally, make sure it is always clear which character is speaking.

Chapter Sixteen

Show Don't Tell

All editors advise their authors *to show, not tell*. What this means is that, instead of writing long paragraphs of explanation or description, you should dramatise what happens or your characters' traits. In other words, do not tell the reader that a particular character is vain or selfish, but show your audience that they behave in a vain or selfish way. Of course, as with all aspects of writing, there are not any absolute rules or correct ways of doing this because exposition and description can play useful roles in your narrative. You must decide what is right for your novel and the story you have to tell.

However, do bear in mind that extended explanation or description tends to be more difficult for your reader to absorb and also substantially slows the pace of the story. You may use either of them exactly for this purpose sometimes and it can be quite appropriate if you seek to vary the pace of your book. However, on occasions when the events or characters you are writing about are immediately important to your story, it will probably be more effective to show the action or behaviour to the reader.

This is true not only of explanation and character description but also physical description. There is nothing wrong with a short physical description of a person, object or setting, but it is often more effective to find a dramatic way of sharing the information with your reader. Perhaps you might have a character comment on another's physical appearance, or by dramatising how a character reacts to something or a setting as opposed to describing a house as neglected or in need of repair, your character might rub their fingers through flaking paintwork.

Take time now to review your first chapter and consider any long pieces of explanation or description and think about whether they need to be there. To this end, consider if they are vital to your story or whether you can dramatise them and make them more easily understood by your reader. Also, if you are describing a character, think about whether you can dramatise their behaviour or give an illustration of the qualities you are explaining to your reader. Equally, when you are making a description of the appearance of one of your characters, the setting or something being used in the story, find a more dramatic way to explain the information.

Go through your whole manuscript, using that first chapter as a template and follow the suggestions made in this and earlier chapters all the way through your book. It will take time and concentration, but it is imperative if your work is to be in as good shape as possible when you submit it for consideration by an agent or publisher.

Chapter Seventeen

Preparing Your Submission

Following completion of the revisions suggested in the previous chapters, you should have edited your book to the point where you feel it is ready for submission. You want to identify potential targets for your submission, and, if you have not already done so, produce a submission plan showing your priority targets.

Name of Publisher / Agent	Contact Name	Address	Reason for Targeting (e.g., current authors/ titles)	Submission Requires

After you have worked through your manuscript so closely, hopefully you will feel that it is as commercial as it can be. It is possible you have even changed your views about the genre of your novel and the target audience or likely readership. This may apply to age group for children's books. You may also have revised how your work compares to that of other authors. In light of this, consider whether your priority targets for submission should be altered.

When you have decided on your final list of submission targets, you should proceed to sort out your submission package. Whether you are submitting to an agent or a publisher, it is imperative that you follow their specific guidelines and requirements for submission. Each will have different requirements but often, these will include: a synopsis of your manuscript, a sample extract from the novel and a covering letter.

You can find the precise details of the relevant submission requirements on the agent's or publisher's website. Make sure you read and follow these carefully. The agent or publisher will not amend their demands just for you. Also make sure the agent or publisher you have targeted is accepting submissions at the time you want to contact them. Check that they are interested in receiving submissions from authors in your genre.

Agents are often specific about the genres they do not represent but sometimes do not specify their preferred genres. However, in larger agencies, each agent will probably specialise in particular genres and may also accept direct submissions. This will usually be detailed on the agency's website. You need to think about every part of your submission package.

Not every agent or publisher requires a synopsis as part of the early submission, but it is often requested at this point. Most will certainly ask for a synopsis at some point during the submission process so make sure you have one prepared. Indeed, it is helpful to have more than one prepared as the length of the required synopsis can vary widely.

Some agents and publishers unhelpfully require a synopsis but do not indicate their preferred length. Traditionally, agents and publishers will accept quite a long synopsis that might be up to 4000 words. In the absence of detailed instructions, you should probably ensure that your submission package includes a long synopsis of this type along with a 'blurb'. This is a much more condensed description of the story of no more than one or two paragraphs such as would ultimately be printed on the back of the published book to entice readers to buy the novel.

Of course, the publishing world has changed a great deal in the last twenty years. Agents and publishers are increasingly busy, and the accessibility of on-line submissions has increased the number of manuscripts that are sent to them. Many agents and publishers struggle to work through the *slush piles* of unsolicited manuscripts they receive. They are able only to give a limited time to considering whether a submission is worth taking further.

If an agent or publisher does ask for a short synopsis but without stating how long it should be, they are likely to be looking for a piece of about 1-2 pages and definitely not more than 1000 words. If they require a synopsis but do not indicate a preferred length at all, it is safer to send a short synopsis in the first instance. If they are really interested in your manuscript, they will ask to see the full manuscript and probably a detailed synopsis later.

You should already have prepared a first draft of your long synopsis for your purposes. Now you need to shape that into a synopsis that is appropriate to include in your submission package in either long or short forms. In truth, you are most likely to submit only the short synopsis initially. Nevertheless, it is worth having the longer version prepared and ready to send if requested. In the event that your book is accepted by an agent or publisher, you will no doubt find the various lengths of your synopsis are useful. Perhaps an agent might want to send a longer version of the synopsis to potential publishers, or you might find it helpful when you are briefing cover designers or even for marketing purposes.

Now consider how you can make the synopsis suitable for submission. Be aware that a short synopsis is basically a sales pitch. It is a longer version of the blurb that will appear on the back of your book. It is a document intended to engage the interest of the agent or publisher you send it to. The longer synopsis is likely to be read only when that interest has been secured, so it can be a more factual version of the story.

The synopsis must set out the story your book tells in the order in which it occurs. Therefore, if you have used flashbacks, place these where they occur in the story and if the tale is told over different time frames, you must make sure that these are clear in the narrative of the synopsis. You must show the story holds together and makes sense. It is important that the agent or publisher can see that it is well structured and that the pace is good. You need to show, also, that your story has a satisfactory conclusion. What you need to do is to give the agent or publisher confidence that you have sustained the quality of your opening chapters throughout the whole book

It is also important that your synopsis introduces your key characters and gives the agent or publisher an understanding of their backgrounds, motivations and personalities. There is no point in providing long character descriptions. They will not be read. But do provide key background details and information relating to the current roles of the characters. It is also useful to give an illustration of their personal qualities.

Your synopsis must be readable in its own right. It is a factual summary of the novel, but it must be interesting and exciting enough to provide the agent or publisher with an idea of what the book is like. It should give an account of the whole story. This means that you do not withhold the ending nor the final twist. The agent or publisher must know that the story works. This can be irritating for writers, especially if the book is a crime novel or thriller. It is easier to make a twist believable in a novel, when you can distract the reader with red herrings and misdirection, than in the limited space of a bare bone synopsis. Here your clever twist may appear less credible. There is not another way around this, except to reflect, as accurately as you can, how you deal with this in your novel. Bear in mind that agents and publishers will be aware of this and will take account of it when they review your submission. If your opening few pages indicate to them that you write well, then they will probably give you a little leeway in terms of how you handle the rest of the book.

Make sure your long synopsis accurately represents your novel in so far as it relates to the detail of its narrative, the structure and its order. It should also be clear, readable and reflect the tone of your book especially in terms of its pace. It is worth getting someone else to read your synopsis and give feedback on it. You, of course, will know your story inside out and back to front, so what is obvious to you will not necessarily be clear to a third party who is unfamiliar with it. The synopsis must also supply a clear grasp of your main characters.

As you have finished preparing your long synopsis, you will realise how challenging that has been. However, preparing a short synopsis is even harder. It is easier to write if you have already got the long version in front of you to work from. You should now work to reduce your synopsis to less than 1000 words.

It will not take you long to work out that this means you must remove a great deal of the detail of your story from the long synopsis to prepare the short synopsis.

The easiest way to do this is to study your long synopsis and highlight only the key plot and character points. You must decide what it is the agent or publisher must know about your story. To do this you have to provide a clear summary of your core narrative and so the synopsis must tell the outline of the whole story including the twist and ending. It is always tempting to leave the ending hanging. You would certainly do this in the blurb on the back of the published version because that would intrigue the reader. Indeed, best-selling author Karen Campbell did exactly that when making her early submissions, but her debut novel, *The Twilight Time*, was so strong she secured representation despite this. Few authors are this fortunate. Ensure that, even in this shorter synopsis, any agent or publisher reading it will be convinced that you can bring your novel to a satisfactory conclusion.

The agent or publisher who receives your synopsis must understand your main characters. You will not have space to provide a great deal of information, so you must find a way of reducing the description of the characters into one or two sentences. You can afford to tell and show. You can describe one of your characters as 'enthusiastic' or 'jaded'. You do not have to dramatise the qualities. But, if you do, you must make sure that you introduce some of your key characters in your beginning chapters. This will show the agent or publisher that you have the skill to present them effectively.

The short synopsis is more of a *sales pitch* than the longer version. Your aim is to capture the imagination of the agent or publisher. It must also give them an idea of how they will be able to sell your book to readers.

Even with this very tight word count, you must be able to demonstrate how your manuscript builds suspense, shows emotions and whatever else you are aiming to do.

This is certainly not easy and you may well find that your synopsis drifts into clichéd phrases such as *with time-running out* or *as the body count builds,* so do try to concentrate on the parts that distinguish the plot, characters or setting of your novel from others. Try to choose original phrases that capture the atmosphere of your novel. It may help to start by looking at back cover blurbs of books that most closely resemble your novel, in terms of genre, setting or overall tone. Also, think about the way the books have been described. You must not duplicate the wording used for other books, nor would you want to. However, it may be useful to use it as a prompt to find short and effective ways of describing your work.

When you have had an opportunity to consider how best to word your short synopsis, try to produce a synopsis of no more than 1000 words. Make sure that this gives a short outline of your book. Include major sub-plots and set out the story in the order that it is told in your novel including the ending. You should introduce the main characters describing their personalities, how they fit into the story and their motivation for their actions. Also, ensure that the tone and pace of your novel is properly reflected in such a way that agents and publishers will be interested and want to read more.

Some agents and publishers still accept submissions in hard copy but the overwhelming majority look for contact by e-mail. Your submission should include a short covering letter and it really should be short, certainly not more than one page.

Make sure the letter is business-like. You should include a brief description of your book, including the genre and sub-genre: crime novel, police procedural. Mention the setting and your main characters and last, but by no means least, include an elevator pitch for the novel. This is critical. It tells the recipient why your book is distinctive and worth reading.

An *elevator pitch* is traditionally said to be what you would say if you attempted to sell your book to an agent, a publisher or even a reader if you were in a lift with them and only had the time between floors to get them interested. It basically requires you to sell your book in a couple of sentences. So, you really have to think about what it is that will make an agent or publisher want to accept working with you on your book rather than any of the many others that come across their desk.

If you struggle to pinpoint the unique selling point of your story, ask yourself whether it is ready for submission at all. Agents and publishers must have a *hook*, a point of interest that will allow them to sell your novel to other people. So, naturally, the more you give them to work with, the more likely they are to accept your submission. Equally, if your story is not distinctive, you need to go back to the drawing board and work on it further. This does not mean that the book has to be completely unique and original. Agents and publishers want books that are in some way different from others on the market but, especially with a novel from a debut author, also one that offers some familiarity to prospective readers.

When you are describing the story, if you are able to say that it is likely to appeal to readers who like other named authors feel free to do that, if the comparison is reasonable. At the same time, you must persuade the agent or publisher that your book offers something additional and distinctive.

Lastly, you must include very brief biographical details about yourself in the covering letter. Focus on information that is pertinent to the submission. Perhaps mention your writing career to date including details of short stories or pieces of non-fiction that you have had published. Do not forget to mention other types of writing experience and details of awards or prizes you have received. Also tell the recipient about the relevant elements from your career that are worthy of mention. This might include a previous job or place you have lived that has been material to the writing of your novel.

Make sure your biography is not more than a few lines long and only includes relevant details. It does have several uses. The agent or publisher will be reassured that you have some skill even if you only have writing experience in entirely different types of pieces. It is also worth considering that many submissions contain very poor grammar, punctuation and spelling. If your cover letter is presented in a business-like way it will encourage the agent or publisher to take your submission more seriously and the letter has done at least part of its job.

Also include anything that is particularly interesting in your past life, even if it is not writing related, any agent or publisher will see that as a hook that could be used to help sell your work. Of course, that is only a little part of the puzzle, and the fact that you were a detective in a major incident team, or a reformed axe murderer does not mean you can write a good crime novel. However, it is something else that helps to make you stand out from the crowd and attract the interest of the agent or publisher. It may be that little thing that encourages them to give your manuscript a second glance.

Your covering letter should be factual, simple, polite and succinct. Agents and publishers are incredibly busy people, so use short paragraphs and consider using bullet points so they can skim through it quickly and get the idea of the points you are trying to make. Do not apologise for your work but on the other hand do not appear conceited. Definitely do not try any gimmicks to try to get attention. Agents and publishers are professional people, and therefore will always look for professionalism in submissions they receive.

Most agents and publishers will ask you to submit an extract from the beginning of your book. This is often the first three chapters or a certain number of pages or a specific wordcount. Do not be tempted to send anything other than the precise extract requested. Sometimes you may feel that an extract from later in the book has more impact or better represents the story. However, if the beginning of the book is not good enough to make the agents or publishers want to read more, it will not hold the interest of a reader either and it needs rewriting.

You should have polished your book already to the point where you are content that it is ready for submission. In fact, the opening extract has probably been polished to within an inch of its life and should be in good shape. Nevertheless, it is worth rereading it once more. This time consider if it is effective as an advertisement for the novel. Make sure the opening chapters grab the reader's attention and make them want to read on.

It is not only that your opening scene should be dramatic or unexpected, although that will help. You must also engage the reader's attention by including details that the reader will see develop later in the novel. This may be an unexplained incident or an argument between characters. You can interest the reader by moving the story between happenings or settings that are apparently unconnected. This will pique the reader's curiosity and mean they want to know how these will be linked as the story progresses. The reader can be encouraged to read on because they want to know more about an unexpected happening, an interesting character, or an unusual setting. It is not unusual for openings to contain several of these.

So, do ensure that the opening sufficiently introduces your main characters, and encourages the reader to want to find out more about them. You do not have to introduce all the main characters in the opening few scenes, but you should introduce your lead protagonist and a number of the other main characters. You also want to try to make sure that the reader gets a good feeling for the cast of characters that will tell the story and get an impression of how they interact. Include some moments that show the different personalities and how they react to each other. If some of the characters have distinctive mannerisms or interesting backstories, provide some indication of these. You do not want to reveal all the secrets at this point but give the reader enough information to interest them and make them want to read on.

The opening chapters must be comprehensible in their own right. This does not mean that everything in the opening section needs to be clearly explained and understandable. You want to give the reader reasons to continue reading, and in part that may be by intriguing them with as yet unexplained events, behaviours or connections. However, if the reader is not sure what is happening, they may not read on. The reader needs to realise what is happening, although they may not yet know why or what the consequences are. Likewise, if an agent or publisher struggles to understand your opening chapters or, if they think a reader would not pursue the story, they are likely to reject your manuscript rather than putting any effort into trying to make sense of your novel.

Try to read the beginning of your novel again as if you were reading it for the first time. Be honest about it and consider whether you find your characters engaging and interesting and want to know more about them. If not, a rewrite is needed. Equally, if the narrative is not exciting or intriguing to you, no reader will be interested either. Make sure it is clear what is happening and that you would want to read on. If your thoughts on these topics are negative or you are not confident about your work, then your novel is still not ready to submit.

You may not want to admit this, but you have only one opportunity to impress any agent or publisher and, if you have doubts, review the opening chapters until you are truly as satisfied as possible that you will make that first impression count.

Now comes the practical matter of formatting your novel. As mentioned above, most agents and publishers now accept on-line submissions. As a result of this there is a tendency not to be as particular about formatting as there was when hard copy submissions were the norm. You need to submit your submission in a professional manner and make sure that it is easy for the recipient to read.

The starting point is the submission guidelines stated by the agent or publisher. Some do not have particular guidelines, but most do, and you should follow these precisely. Apart from that, apply common sense.

Usually, agents or publishers ask for manuscripts to be double-spaced with a good margin on all sides to allow them to make notes or comments. Even if it is not specified, it is good practice, although some are happy with 1.5 spacing and will probably read the book electronically anyway.

At the front of your submission, you will have a title page. This will have your name and address and other contact details including your telephone number or e-mail address on it. Even if this information appears in other places in your submission, perhaps in the covering letter, try to make the recipient's job easy. You want them to feel warmly towards your submission, so number the pages and include the title and author name in a header or footer on each page.

It is possible that the recipient will print off your submission, so make it easily identifiable. If you use a pen name, cross-reference to your given name on both the title page and in the covering letter. Double-check your manuscript to make sure that your grammar, spelling and punctuation are accurate. The agent or publisher will not expect your work to be perfectly proofread, but they expect it to be presented properly.

Chapter Eighteen

Submitting Your Work

The final and definitely the most nerve-wracking stage of all you have done so far is to submit your book to agents or publishers. In times gone by, writers were told to submit their work to one agent or publisher at a time. They then had to wait for a reply before submitting to someone else. This meant that the submission process lasted a very long time. Now, most agents and publishers realise that it is unreasonable to expect a writer to wait weeks or even months between each of their submissions. Having said this, do not send out a blanket submission to many agents or publishers at the same time as that will not help the quality of your submissions nor your ability to keep track of them.

If you select the most compatible agents or publishers for your work and target them, your submission is more likely to find favour. Initially submit to no more than five. If any of these are large agencies or publishing houses, make sure you have identified the most appropriate person within the company, to submit your work to and address your submission to them personally, unless the submission guidelines state otherwise. If you do this, spell their name correctly and use their correct title or honorific. Agents and commissioning editors are professional in their dealings and will treat your submission professionally. However, you will not endear yourself or your work to them if you give the impression that your attitude is careless before they have even started to read your manuscript.

Writers often complain about how long it takes for agents or publishers to get back to them about submissions. The truth of the matter is that they are inundated with unsolicited submissions. Even small publishing houses receive hundreds every week and reviewing submissions is only one small part of an agent's or publisher's work. Most of their time is spent taking care of the interests of their clients and authors. They review new submissions when they have time, but, realistically, this work is lower on their priority list, so you must be patient. Do not chase recipients of your work, especially before it is reasonable to do so. That means being willing to wait for at least three months. Some agents and publishers state in their guidelines that they do not provide rejections. In these cases, if you have not heard from them after six months, assume no news is bad news.

Many agents and publishers do send out rejection letters, or more likely now, e-mails. Bearing that in mind, if you have not received anything from them after about three months, you could reasonably send a polite note asking if the submission was received. Remember you must be polite, not only is it good manners, it also makes good sense because if the agent or publisher is considering your work and is minded to accept it, a rude e-mail is not going to persuade them to proceed.

Also be aware that the publishing world is a small one, and people move from company to company within the industry. If you get a reputation as being difficult or unpleasant to work with, that will be difficult to get rid of. The submission process can be frustrating, but it is part of the writer's journey and you must just live with it. Only the very fortunate are successful with their early submissions. The initial replies you get will most likely be rejections and, in most instances, they will not tell you why your submission has been rejected. Most agents and publishers do not have time to give individual writers feedback for the manuscripts they reject. You are likely to get a proforma note or e-mail which simply tells you the manuscript is not right for our list at this time. It is frustrating, because it does not tell you whether your submission was a near miss or a complete flop. But it is all part of the process. However, it might be useful to know that almost as many submissions are declined because of a poor synopsis or covering letter as are rejected because of the content of the extract from the story.

If you are lucky and do receive feedback, treasure that and consider it carefully. Feedback from an agent or publisher, even when it accompanies a rejection is useful because it is the opinion of someone who accepts and rejects manuscripts for a living. They are a professional in a highly competitive field so, If they mention changes that you could make, pay attention. It may be useful, not just for the present submission but also anything you submit in future. You may not fully agree with the comments but think about why they felt the way they did. You may decide not to accept the feedback but do consider changes you can make to address the concerns that have been raised.

Feedback from an agent or publisher at this stage is also useful because it indicates that they have taken your work seriously. Even if they have not asked to see more or the full manuscript, your work has been given more than a passing glance.

In truth, most submissions will be rejected before the agent or publisher has finished reading the first page. It will only take them that long to deduce that the work does not meet their standards and never will, no matter how much work is put into it. Therefore, if the agent or publisher has read your submission for long enough to be able to provide feedback, then they have seen something worth considering. They have probably seen that you write to a reasonable standard, or that there is quite a good and commercial idea in your story. They have engaged with your writing to this limited extent and that is a step towards success.

You should, therefore, accept even negative feedback in a positive spirit. Take it seriously and before making further submissions, consider your novel again and make any changes you can in response to the criticism. This will improve your chances of success in the future.

Many agents or publishers are actually loathe to provide feedback, partly because of their lack of time but also because they do not want to drift into a state of redundant intimacy that results from corresponding with a writer whom they reject. If an agent or publisher does give feedback to you, accept it but do not treat it as an invitation to respond further unless they have invited you to do so.

Even if your book is excellent, you will get many rejections and, even if you have read every tale about the many rejections initially received by writers who are now most successful authors, it will be discouraging. As many agents and publishers are not able to give feedback, you usually will not know if your manuscript has been rejected because it is not quite up to standard or because it really is not at all suitable for publication. Still, you need to keep your spirits up and believe in yourself. If you have trusted, experienced beta readers who say that the book has merit and you have critically dealt with the feedback they offered and the recommendations in this book, then you should carry on with your story. Do this even if you feel discouraged.

Remember, publishing is a very subjective business and in truth nobody really knows exactly what makes a book successful. Indeed, most popular novels have really come from nowhere. These novels sometimes create or redefine a genre as they rise through the lists. They have often been turned down many times before finding success. Other books that are similar may then be written. However, publishers will still seek books that tap into the same audience but are distinctive enough to make their own impact.

Agents and publishers seek submissions that are original, but which can successfully be sold to the reading public by referencing to other authors or specific novels. Be aware, they will not accept your submission unless it meets the quality of writing, narrative and characterisation that they are looking for. But even if it does meet their standards, they will also ask themselves if it is saleable. They must feel keen about it, and how they can market it to potential readers. At this point it is not about the quality of your submission. It is really about how well the agent or publisher thinks your book will sell. Now their opinion becomes most subjective.

They must go with their instinct and if they love your book, they will feel they can sell it easily to others. However, if they liked it well enough but did not feel it was entirely to their taste, they may feel that they cannot do it justice when trying to sell it. This is simply a personal opinion. It is important to realise that to get your book published requires not only talent, but also persistence, resilience and luck.

The more you put into the first three of these qualities, the more likely you are to make your own luck. You are highly unlikely to secure an agent or publisher who loves your work the first time you submit your book. Indeed, it may take you ten, twenty or even more submissions to find a compatible agent or publisher. If your work has merit, you are likely to find success eventually. Should you get a positive response perhaps in the form of constructive feedback, a request for the full manuscript or even a positive note and not just a *pro forma* response know that you are well on your way. It means the book has caught the interest of the agent or publisher. Give yourself that credit, even if the outcome is a rejection at the end of the day. However, do not get over excited because of a few positive words, but do treat a positive response as a step in the right direction.

If you get repeated rejections, but you believe your novel is good, ask yourself if it is your submission that is unmarketable. Consider whether the submission is really suited to promoting your book in the market. Make sure you spend your time producing a submission that will attract an agent or publisher's attention in your novel. It is also too easy to be so blinded by your own work that you forget to consider whether it will appeal to a large enough number of readers to be commercial.

If you begin to consider that possibility, return to re-analyse your manuscript. Think about which genre and sub-genre your book falls into. Consider whether it is reflective of the novels by any other writer and, bearing that in mind, ask yourself which readers you think will form your target market. If you do not have a market, your book will not sell in sufficient quantities to be of interest to an agent or publisher.

You must be honest and consider the negative points in your manuscript as well as the positive qualities. Consider your novel from the point of view of an agent trying to pitch it to a publisher, or of a publisher trying to sell it to possible readers. If you struggle to categorise the genre of your novel, agents and publishers will have exactly that issue too. If the book does not fit fully into one genre, it is probable that an agent or publisher will have the same problem about how they can sell it to readers.

Equally, if your novel is reminiscent of books by authors who are not selling well or whose work only has a restricted following then you must understand that it is unlikely to appeal to agents or publishers because it will not be easy to market.

Another possible problem can be that far from being too unusual to sell, it may be that your work is far *too* like books by another author. If this is the case, there may not be enough room in the market for a new author writing the same type of book.

Lastly, imagine people spending their hard-earned money to buy your book and think why they would want to buy it. Be honest and consider whether they are more likely to buy a paperback book or an e-book. You need to know the sort of readers they would be. You must know your target market and whether they are mostly male or female, how old they are and think about whether they are readers of an established genre. The reason you need to know this is so that you know what your audience expects from the book. Readers are more likely to buy your novels if they think they know what to expect and that they are likely to enjoy it.

If, when you have thought about all of that, you still believe that your book is marketable, then continue with your submissions as they are. If you have doubts, it is worth reviewing the manuscript and your submission as a whole. This will be a most unwelcome suggestion, but to have the possibility of success after numerous rejections, think about whether there is something you can amend to make the book more marketable, or to make agents or publishers more likely to want to sell your novel.

Perhaps you will have to make small changes, or your work might even involve a major rewrite. It is even possible that you decide to abandon this book, certainly for the time being, and start again, this time writing something easier to sell.

There is no doubt that to go down this road would be a really hard decision but it is a better course of action than flogging a dead horse and continuing to make submissions that attract no interest. Many successful authors have unpublished manuscripts that were never submitted or were rejected when they were submitted.

Chapter Nineteen

Submitting the Full Manuscript

Those who decide to abandon a manuscript and start again are faced with a worst-case scenario and, honestly, many do not start again but turn their attention to different endeavours.

It is much more positive to think about, even after numerous rejections, finding an agent or publisher who wants to see your whole manuscript. That is a really exciting time and an amazing achievement. No agent or publisher will ask to see your full novel unless they are truly interested in your submission. So, if you are asked for your full manuscript, you must send it as soon as you can. That is why your draft requires to have been completed before you even start sending submissions to agents and publishers.

It is tempting, when you get to this point and receive such interest to view it as a make or break time in your writing career. Do not keep refining and polishing the draft to try to make it completely perfect. Feel free to read it over one more time and if the agent or publisher has given you any feedback on the opening chapters it might be sensible to make the suggested changes before sending the full manuscript to the agent or publisher.

You should not delay for long before you respond to the request. It is possible that, if they have requested a full manuscript, the agent is aware of a publisher who is looking for your kind of novel. Alternatively, it may be that a publisher who has shown an interest in your book is looking to fill an immediate space in their schedule or to enlarge their list of authors and capitalise on the success of novels that have recently been published. Even if that is not so, the agent or publisher is interested in your manuscript *right now*. That interest may have evaporated in just a few weeks because they may receive an alternative interesting piece of work and give that priority over yours. Do not send out your opening chapters until you have the full book finished and the manuscript available to send to interested parties. Put simply, if you cannot send your full manuscript upon request, any parties with a potential interest in your book are likely to lose interest quickly.

However, if you have received a request for your full manuscript, you should not expect to get a speedy reply. The agent or publisher who has expressed an interest will want to take time to read your work fully. While some of them, particularly in larger firms, will probably also need or want to talk to their colleagues, but other agents will be able to make a decision on your submission alone. Publishers almost always make a collective decision. In larger companies, a commissioning editor will need to discuss marketing or sales with colleagues in those departments before a final decision is made. A good commissioning editor will want make sure that there is excitement for the book across all departments before taking it on because, if the marketing or sales staff are not interested in your book, it is not likely to be promoted successfully. Just be aware that because of this there is likely to be a delay before you get any response. Also, even if the initial recipient likes your book, it may not be accepted, and this is most upsetting so be aware that you must overcome many obstacles to become a successful author. This is the way the industry works. On the plus side, when your novel is accepted by an agent or publisher you will have the whole firm helping it to become a success.

You should not be upset if an agent or publisher wants to see your full manuscript but ultimately rejects it. There could be many reasons for this. Perhaps they find your full book does not live up to the opening chapters or your synopsis or it is not distinctive enough. Alternatively, your novel was just not acceptable to their colleagues. At this point, you may well get more feedback from the agent or publisher. Often this is just a sentence or two telling you why they will not be representing you. If you are lucky, you might get some advice as to how you could improve your manuscript before you resubmit it. If you do get feedback, accept it graciously and take it seriously. Think about how you should respond to it before you submit your work to them or submit it somewhere else. If you do not agree with their opinion, remember that it is the view of a professional who could have accepted your book.

Basically, when submitting to agents and publishers you must be patient. You should continue sending out your submissions and working through your target professionals. Remember always to pay attention to the literary marketplace. There are often especially fast changes notified on-line and in writers forums. New publishers and imprints from existing publishers are set up all the time and this means the opportunities to be published are increasing. Not all successful authors were lucky with their first book. Ian Rankin had published three novels under the name of Jack Harvey and seven more Rebus novels as Ian Rankin before his book, *Black and Blue*, was recognised with a Gold Dagger Award by the Crime Writers' Association in the UK. Thereafter, his novels became increasingly popular.

If you believe that you have reached the end of the possibilities for submitting your novel, then consider setting this book aside and start writing a completely different story.

This will be a heart-rending decision but if you are determined to become an author you must accept the rough parts of the journey with the smooth. It does not matter if your book is excellent, if it does not fit into the market at the time you are submitting then you should try to write something completely different.

Chapter Twenty

Getting or Not Getting a Deal

There may well come a time when your book is finally accepted, and you do your happy dance around the living room. However, before you celebrate wildly, you would be wise to ensure that the offer you have received is what you expected. If you have received an offer from a respected, established agent or publisher that is well thought of, you are not likely to have too much to worry about. Nevertheless, you will want to check the contract carefully so that you know that you are happy with it. It is likely to be a contract that conforms to the industry standards.

You may want to examine the contract more carefully if it has come from a newer publisher.

You are keen to be published, but you do want to be treated fairly. You might want to try to get advice from other published authors you know. They may be able to guide you about typical royalty rates. Be aware that these do vary not only from publisher to publisher, but also from author to author. Some publishers take different approaches to different kinds of publications including hardback books, paperback books, e-books, audiobooks, and foreign rights so check that the contract being offered to you is within an acceptable industry range.

Traditionally, publishers offered an advance on royalties. This is a payment made to the author in advance of publication, but which is reclaimed by the publisher from the royalty earnings.

Today, many newer publishers offer a royalties-only arrangement and therefore often pay a higher royalty rate. This is not really a problem. Although, if an advance is paid, it may be helpful to the author and perhaps encourages the publisher to assist in promotion of the book. However, the advances paid are usually quite small now and therefore do not make a huge difference. Even large advances referred to on the rumour mill are not what they seem to be. They may apply to contracts for more than one book and are often paid in instalments. Typically, payments are made on signing the contract, on delivering the manuscript and again on publication. Actual payments received, therefore, may be quite small and also paid over a long period of time. Traditional publishers usually pay royalties only twice a year whereas newer publishers who do not pay advances often make quarterly payments.

If you are not used to reading contracts, it is sensible to have someone to check the contract for you. That is a perfectly reasonable thing to do as you want to know that there are not any damaging clauses or unexpected restrictions imposed on you.

If you have an agent, they will negotiate the contract for you and check it over. If you do not have an agent, you should consider joining the Society of Authors https://www.societyofauthors.org/ in Britain or The Authors' Guild https://www.authorsguild.org/ in America. It is possible to join both of these organisations as an emerging author if a publishing contract has been offered to you even if you have not signed it. These organisations will be able to provide advice on the contract and its terms.

Under no circumstances should you pay a publisher to produce your novel. No reputable agent or publisher will ever ask for any upfront payment from an author.

Normal practice would be for you to pay your agent a commission from your royalties. Equally, publishers invest a great deal in the preparation, production and distribution of your book. It is usual for them to take a share of the royalty payments to cover their expenses. If you receive a request for payment by an agent to review your work or to represent you, walk away. If a publisher demands payment from you to cover the design or production of your novel, again, walk away.

You must decide, bearing in mind the advice you get, if the offer you have received is good. If the royalty rates and other details are acceptable, also consider the track record of the agent or publisher and find out what their reputation is like in the industry and with the authors in their stable. Do not be shy about asking questions about anything relating to the contract if you do not understand something. They will not be aggrieved but will be happy to explain their terms and will want you to be satisfied with them.

There are many issues you may want to clarify before you sign the contract. Be sure you know which other authors are on the list of your agent or publisher and how they intend to sell your novel. Also, ask how the agent intends to work with you.

If you have been accepted by a publisher remember to ask how much time they intend to spend marketing and distributing your book and how much time they expect you to invest in that part of the business. Remember, if you are required to spend too much time publicising your first book, you may not have time to write the second.

Whatever you do, do not have unrealistic expectations. No agent or publisher can promise that your book will be successful. Issues may arise along the way from acceptance to publication and even after that. So, you must be able to approach the business with your agent or publisher with reciprocal understanding and effort. That way your association will be most fruitful.

If you decide to accept the offer, you must tell any agents or publishers to whom you have sent your submission. It is a courtesy, and it is worth thinking about the fact that the publishing sector is quite small and if you create goodwill early, it cannot do you any harm as your career progresses. Once you have done that and signed the contract, you can, at last, open a bottle of wine or have a frothy coffee.

If, however, no agent or publisher is willing to represent your book, remember that your success depends not only on talent but also good luck. Many good books are never accepted by the traditional arm of the industry. Alternatively, you may decide that traditional publishing does not suit you or your book because the novel does not have a wide enough appeal, or simply because you want to keep maximum control over your work.

This may make it worthwhile to think about self-publishing. In the past, to self-publish was a sign of failure but that is no longer true. Some very popular writers have decided to self-publish and built very lucrative careers. These include L J Ross and Catriona King. Some writers self-publish first and then move over to a traditional publisher as E L James did. Other authors mix traditionally published novels with self-published books and in this way have a hybrid career. You may find you like self-publishing or a hybrid business as it will give you more control over your career.

It is definitely worth thinking about positively, not negatively. Self-publishing is not dealt with in detail in this book. However, let us consider the main issues you must know about if you decide to self-publish.

The hardest thing is that you must be sure that the manuscript is of good quality. Your novel may have been turned down by agents and publishers because you were unlucky, but it could be that your work was not of a high enough standard. You need to be honest with yourself.

It does not mean that your book has no value, but it could require significant extra work. There is no bar to you self-publishing the book as it is and certainly there are many sub-standard self-published books on the market. However, if you want to be successful, you must make sure that your novel is as good as it possibly can be. To self-publish successfully, it would be sensible to engage the services of a professional editor who will give you an honest, expert opinion on the quality of your work. They will also be able to help you get the novel into a good state. But do bear in mind that this will incur an expense of possibly several hundred pounds.

While self-publishing will allow you to do some of the production of your book yourself, you should not think of it as an easy or cheap option. However, if you are to do it properly, think about how much you are willing and able to do yourself. It may be worthwhile to budget for the editing of your manuscript because this is your responsibility. Consider what type and level of editing your manuscript requires. It is certainly worthwhile investing in an experienced copyeditor. Again, proofreading is your responsibility. It is extremely difficult to proofread your own work and so you may find it is sensible to invest to have this done by a professional.

If you plan to self-publish through Amazon, they provide helpful technical support that will assist you with the layout and production of your book. It is possible to learn how to prepare your manuscript for production as an e-book or a paperback book or both. Of course, someone who is experienced will do it far more quickly and to a higher standard than you can.

Cover design is very important. We are told not to judge a book by its cover, but we all do it. Therefore, making sure the cover of your book is appealing to your target market is important. Support and resources are available an appealing, professional-looking cover design is critical to the success of your book, especially if you are a debut author. A designer can be secured relatively inexpensively, and it is worthwhile to invest in the best cover design that you can.

This all needs not only time, but money and you must think about the amount you are willing and able to spend. It may depend on what type of book you have written and the level of your own skills.

You also need to make other decisions. Consider which platforms you want to use for your book. In this regard, Amazon is certainly the self-publishing market leader. It also offers substantial benefits if you only publish on Amazon, however often writers want their books to be available on a variety of platforms.

Marketing your book is also important and, while you will be involved in this if you publish traditionally or self-publish, the responsibility lies entirely with you if you self-publish. There are various social media platforms that offer free or inexpensive ways of attracting the attention of your target market. You can do this by advertising directly and by joining readers' forums. Other popular marketing options that exist are blog tours that you arrange with bloggers interested in the type of book you have written. You should also have an author website, social media accounts and perhaps a podcast or YouTube channel where you can promote your novel and, if you are willing to devote the time to it, establish a mailing list and post regular information, content and contests that will help you to build it up and add followers.

Some of these marketing choices involve no financial cost at all. Others can involve you in some or even considerable cost. It really depends on whether you are willing and able to spend time promoting your book yourself or pay to secure the assistance of others to do so on your behalf.

Successful self-published authors usually achieve their high level of sales through an investment of both time and money in their marketing. Marketing and promotion of your book is part of an author's job.

Seeing your book on the shelf of a bookstore or library shelf is exciting. Seeing somebody reading your book on a train is exhilarating and finding your book is a best seller is remarkable. The road to becoming a successful author is not easy, but it is rewarding. Enjoy the journey!

Made in the USA
Monee, IL
17 June 2020